Dear Miranda,

Happy 17th Birthday
Gorgeous and Talented!
Lots of love
Pam and Gary

X X X X X

Dear Miranda,

I0655107

Geisha

Geisha

Text and Original Photography

Kyoko Aihara

CARLTON
BOOKS

THIS A CARLTON BOOK
Design copyright © 1999 Carlton Books Limited
Text and original photography copyright
© 1999 Kyoko Aihara

This edition published by Carlton Books Limited 2000
20 Mortimer Street
London
W1N 7RD

A CIP catalogue for this book is
available from the British Library

ISBN 1 85868 937 6

Executive Editor: Sarah Larter
Art Director: Trevor Newman
Design: Anthony Cohen
Additional Picture Research: Alex Pepper
Production: Janette Davis

Printed and bound in Dubai

Contents

Introduction   6

ONE
Kyoto's Hanamachi Community   8

TWO
Maiko   28

THREE
The Life of a Geiko   42

FOUR
The Maiko and Geiko Look   56

FIVE
Artistic Accomplishments   78

SIX
Banquets and Performances   90

SEVEN
Calendar of Events   104

EIGHT
Modern Life in
the Hanamachis   114

Glossary   124

Index and
Acknowledgements   126

The Past in the Present

In the past, two primary images have been associated with Japan in the Western imagination – Mount Fuji and the lavishly costumed women called geisha. Today, however, the country is more likely to be associated with the brandnames of technological products. The westernization of Japan, which has accelerated since World War Two, has changed its society considerably. It is now rare to come across traditional dance or music in everyday life, and the kimono is worn only on special occasions, such as weddings or at New Year, less so by men than by women. The younger generation is more interested in the piano or guitar than traditional Japanese instruments such as the *shamisen* (a three-stringed instrument), likewise their music of choice is likely to be *yogaku* (western), rather than *hogaku* (traditional Japanese). These days most Japanese sleep in beds, rather than on futons, and eat at tables sitting on chairs. Many homes have only one Japanese-style room carpeted in the traditional manner with straw mats called *tatami*. In contrast, the physical setting of the *hanamachis* – the areas of Japanese cities where the geisha, geiko and maiko live and work – remains, on the whole, as it has been for centuries.

Within the hanamachis, what was once the universal Japanese lifestyle persists, the old culture confined and condensed into small communities. Nowhere is this more true than in the hanamachis of Japan's ancient capital, Kyoto, where, without exception, the *ochayas* (teahouses) remain as they have always been. Every room, for example, retains an alcove called a *tokonoma*, containing traditional *ikebana* flower arrangements and paintings or calligraphy hanging on the wall.

It is in such teahouses that the geisha, geiko and maiko entertain their male guests by dancing, singing ballads and playing traditional musical instruments. A man has to be considerably wealthy to be able to afford to dine in an ochaya, an *ichigen-san* – a chance customer or stranger, will not be admitted to a banquet even if he can afford it: a prospective guest must be invited by someone already acquainted with the teahouse. The world of the hanamachis is unfamiliar to the average Japanese person and is shrouded by a veil of secrecy. Like most Japanese people, I could only imagine what the hanamachis were like until I was allowed inside those in Kyoto to research and photograph this book. I was fortunate enough to meet and interview many of the people who work within the hanamachis, allowing me a fascinating insight into this world.

Because they are among the last remaining links to Japan's past, the hanamachis attract much attention and curiosity. There are many hanamachis

throughout Japan but those in Kyoto are unique. In spite of this uniqueness, very little has been written about this female society, even in Japanese.

In the Western world, the word geisha is understood to describe the women who entertain in the hanamachis. Indeed in most cities and towns where they exist in Japan, this is what they are called. The level of artistic accomplishment varies according to region and the individual. In Kyoto however, where their training is more rigorous, they are referred to as maiko and geiko. The word geisha is used generally by outsiders, unaware of the complexities of Kyoto's hanamachi society and the lengths to which these women go to to improve their art. Throughout this book, which draws on the experiences of Kyoto's female entertainers, the apprentices, who exist only in Kyoto and have no equivalent elsewhere in Japan, are referred to as maiko (woman of dance), while their fully-fledged sisters are called geiko (woman of art). The strict observance of the rules, customs and practices of former days makes these remarkable women the guardians of Japan's cultural heritage.

Kyoto's Hanamachi Community

Take a stroll along Hanamikoji in Kyoto, where the cherry blossom is viewed in the Spring or Shinbashi-dori (New Bridge Street) in the hanamachi of Gion or along similar streets in the hanamachis of Kamishichiken and Miyagawa-cho, and you could be back in the seventeenth century, at the beginning of the Edo Period. Lined with well-maintained traditional houses, the hanamachis resemble scenes from an historical drama. So precious are these areas that certain streets in Gion and Miyagawa-cho have been designated by the local authority as special conservation and restoration areas and efforts are being made to preserve the past in all its former glory.

**Two geiko walking through
the hanamachi of Miyagawa-cho.**

Kyoto's Hanamachi Community

Within the hanamachis of Kyoto are found the ochayas – teahouses where the maiko and geiko entertain. A typical ochaya has several distinct features. There is a sliding lattice door at the entrance on the ground floor and the windows that face out on the first floor are usually covered with a finely woven rattan or bamboo screen. Inside the house, you will find an *ozashiki,* where banquets are held, floored with neatly woven straw mats called tatami, an alcove called a tokonoma with a hanging scroll, decorated with black-and-white characters, well-polished wooden corridors and a small Japanese-style quadrangle.

According to statistics recorded on 31 July 1999, there are 190 ochayas remaining in Kyoto's five hanamachis, employing 195 geiko and 55 maiko. The largest and the most representative, Gion-Kobu, has 83 ochayas, 90 geiko and 20 maiko; the smallest, Gion-Higashi has 11 ochayas, 10 geiko and 5 maiko, though all these numbers fluctuate a little.

A tayu parade in Shimabara at the end of the Meiji period (*c.*1912).

Kyoto's Hanamachis

Kyoto was the capital of Japan for more than a thousand years, until the Meiji Restoration (1868) when Tokyo became the principal city. Many Shinto shrines and Buddhist temples still exist there, as do many old buildings – and the hanamachis, where festivals and ceremonies are held in all their complexity, as they were in centuries gone by. Kyoto has six hanamachis: Gion-Kobu, Gion-Higashi, Ponto-cho, Kamishichiken, Miyagawa-cho and Shimabara. The last of these, however, although Japan's oldest licensed pleasure-quarter, is no longer active and the others are collectively known as the *Gokagai* – meaning the five hanamachis.

There is only one teahouse (known as an *ageya* in this hanamachi), left in Shimabara now. Named Sumiya, it was designated a National Cultural Property in 1952 and has recently been converted into a museum. There is only one *okiya* (lodging house) called wachigai ya, that is also used as an ageya. It is here that the *tayu* – who like the geisha are female entertainers highly trained in art, culture and dress – entertain guests at banquets. Only six tayu remain in Shimabara today. The tayu's dress, hair and make up are more colourful than the geiko's and her teeth are stained black. To entertain, she may play the *kokyu* (Chinese fiddle) or the *ichigenkin* (single-stringed

The entrance to the hanamachi of Shimabara today.

11

instrument) or *sugoroku* (a traditional dice game) or demonstrate *tosenkyo* (fan throwing) – all of which the tayu once performed in the Kyoto Imperial Palace. Today, it is tourists visiting the Sumiya museum who are treated to a traditional tayu show, with the roles of the tayu and their accompanying players performed by professional dancers and instructors.

Shimabara was moved to its present location in 1641 and flourished in the mid-Edo Period as a gathering place for poets. It is here that *haiku*, a school of Japanese poetry called Shimabara Haidan, was formed.

Shimabara was at its height in the Genroku Era (1688–1704), after which time it began to decline. A well-known Japanese novelist, Bakin Takizawa wrote of its deterioration when he visited the area in 1802, describing how the district's mud walls had collapsed, that it was no longer visited because it was too far from the city centre, and that it did not compare with the entertainments offered in Gion.

Gion: The Yasaka shrine, originally called the Gion shrine, is situated at the foot of Higashiyama (East Mountain). The shrine is dedicated to Susano-no-Mikoto, a Shinto god, and is mentioned in the *Kojiki*, the oldest Japanese writing, compiled in 712. Gion has always been a popular place for people to visit, pilgrims and travellers gather at the area's shrines and temples, particularly to see the cherry blossom in spring and the turning leaves in autumn.

In the mid-sixteenth century Gion contained a number of *mizu-jayas* (taverns) that served tea to visitors. One of these, called Kashiwaya, can be seen in historic drawings of the Yasaka shrine, and still stands nearby. The number of taverns increased from the early Edo Period, gradually starting to serve sake, snacks and light meals such as tofu. The houses were enlarged and

The Sumiya teahouse in Shimabara.

A traditional tayu show performed for tourists in the Shimabara district.

LEFT: A geiko goes about her business in Gion.
ABOVE: The distinctive rattan blinds that front an ochaya.

rooms for guests were introduced. It was from these establishments that Gion's ochayas emerged.

In 1665 the ochayas were licensed and moved to a newly built area called Gion-Shinchi (Gion New Land). Subsequently, Gion became Kyoto's largest hanamachi. In 1732 the licensed area was further enlarged to the northern side of what is now Shijo Street. At the same time there was a crackdown on prostitution. In 1813 the geiko and maiko were first licensed as a profession and allowed to work in Gion.

The first half of the nineteenth century was Gion's golden era, when it was a meeting place for men of letters and arts. At the time there were some seven hundred teahouses and more than three thousand geiko and maiko. Before the Meiji Restoration in 1867, the Royalists gathered here because it was safe and inhabitants of the hanamachi were discreet. Because of this, they continued to visit after the Restoration. The first governor of the Kyoto Prefecture tried to maintain Gion's success as Kyoto's prosperity depended on it. The hanamachi flourished in the late nineteenth and early twentieth centuries during the wars with China (1894–5) and Russia (1904), continuing to do so up to the beginning of World War One, with more than 1,000 geiko

and maiko working during this period, some of whom became famous. One geiko, known as Oyuki, was said to have been employed by an American millionaire known as George Morgan for 40,000 yen, equivalent to one hundred million today. Eventually Oyuki married her millionaire.

In 1886 Gion was divided in two, Gion-Kobu and Gion-Otsubu. In 1949 Gion-Otsubu was renamed Gion-Higashi-Shinchi (meaning Eastern New Land) before becoming Gion-Higashi, as it is today.

Like Gion, the hanamachi of **Ponto-cho** is located in the parish of the Yasaka shrine. It is Kyoto's second-largest hanamachi after Gion-Kobu, and comprises a narrow street, stretching from north to south that is approximately 500 metres long by 50 metres wide. The word "Ponto" is not Japanese in origin – it is generally believed to come from the Portuguese "ponta" meaning point. Portugal was the first Western country with which Japan had contact in the mid-sixteenth century. Ponto-cho is also mentioned in the 1682 novel *Koshoku-Ichidai-Otoko* by Saikaku Ihara, the title of which means "a man who has spent his whole life devoting himself to love without ever marrying"– which tells the tale of a protagonist who, having first falling in love at the age of seven, sets sail at sixty for a legendary island of women.

In 1614 the Takase-gawa canal was constructed on the west side of Kyoto's Kamo River. As a result of works completed in 1670, an island was formed between the river and the canal, with an excellent view of Higashiyama. By early in the next century this area, now known as Ponto-cho, had expanded and the busy traffic on the canal had brought many travellers and boatmen to the restaurants, teahouses and inns.

Guests in the establishments of Ponto-cho were entertained by women called *wataboshi*, some of whom worked as prostitutes. At that time, Shimabara was the only licensed quarter in Kyoto and it was at its request that some 1,300 of these entertainers were transferred there.

Before geiko were licensed in Ponto-cho, *haizens* (waitresses) served sake and meals to guests. These waitresses are the predecessors of the present *nakai* who still serve drinks and meals in Japanese-style restaurants and inns. During this period, young girls who lived nearby and were learning how to dance were invited to perform at banquets as an additional entertainment – a role that eventually developed into that of the maiko.

Kamishichiken meaning "seven houses in the upper area", is the oldest remaining active hanamachi in Kyoto. The area originated when seven teahouses were built with material left over from the reconstruction of the Kitano shrine, following a fire during the Muromachi Period. When Shogun Hideyoshi Toyotomi unified Japan in 1582, a grand tea party was held in Kitano where Kamishichiken is now located and the seven teahouses were used to accommodate the guests.

Most of the land in Kamishichiken belongs to a Buddhist convent called Saihoniji where the geiko and maiko of the hanamachi still gather to learn the

ABOVE: A maiko poses outside an ochaya in Kamishichiken, the oldest existing hanamachi in Kyoto.

OPPOSITE: Gion viewed from the Yasaka shrine at the beginning of the Meiji period (above). The Shijo Ohashi bridge over the Kamo River, Meiji period (below).

tea ceremony. Kamishichiken, which prospered in the first half of the
seventeenth century, is in the parish of the Kitano-Tenmangu shrine, which is
dedicated to Minister Michizane Sugawara (845–903), deified after his death
as a champion of learning. The shrine is therefore very popular with students.

There were many shrine maidens at Kitano-Tenmanu who communicated
the god's message and, when grown to womanhood, prophesied in the shrine
or prepared tea in the local teahouses. They were required to be demure and
are said to be the model for the geiko of Kamishichiken. This hanamachi is
situated in the weaving district called Nishijin and its factory and shop owners
have been frequent customers.

Located near Gion on the east bank of the Kamo, **Miyagawa-cho** (Shrine
river ward) derives its name from a the sacred palanquin of the Yasaka shrine
which was traditionally washed in the river's waters.

In 1751 a licence for a teahouse was granted to Miyagawa-cho which,
already having the famous Minamiza kabuki theatre and various playhouses in
its neighbourhood was already a popular area for entertainment.

When female kabuki dancing was prohibited in 1629, *wakashu kabuki*,
performed by young boys, developed, with female roles played by the most

HANAMACHI CRESTS

Every Japanese family has its own crest that appears on both men's and women's formal kimonos, worn on a variety of different occasions. So do the maiko, whose crests are those of their okiya, while the independent geiko have their own. The five hanamachis also have their crests, which always appear on paper lanterns, banners and curtains as well as on the decorations and ornaments used on special occasions, such as festivals and ceremonies.

The crest of Gion Kobu was originally a combination of the initial characters of the eight wards in the Gion hanamachi. The eight characters were linked in a circle around the initial character of Gion. Later, the eight characters were changed to eight *dangos* (dumplings made with rice powder) symbolizing *mitarashi dango*, which historically was served at the *mizu-jayas*.

When Gion was partitioned into Gion-Kobu and Gion-Otsubu, the initial character of Gion was replaced by the character for Kobu in the first case and to the character for Otsubu in the second. However, when Gion-Otsubu was renamed Gion-Higashi in 1944, the initial character was deleted.

Shogun Hideyoshi Toyotomi's praise for the mitarashi dango at the grand tea party in Kitanso when he became Shogun in the sixteenth century led to Kamishichiken adopting the dumpling as its crest.

Ponto-cho's crest was introduced at the first performance of the Kamo River dance festival in 1872, the design based on the plover which frequents the river in winter.

Miyagawa-cho's crest combines three rings to celebrate the joint sponsorship of the Nyokoba school for geiko and maiko – when it became a Prefectural school – by the shrines and temples, local townsmen and the hanamachi.

attractive. This is the origin of *onnagata* in kabuki plays in which the male actor plays in female roles. Unfortunately, before long, the young wakashu kabuki dancers became a sexual target for priests and samurai warriors.

Many young kabuki actors who lived in Miyagawa-cho became well known and some went to Edo to improve their theatrical art. In many cases kabuki actors take their *yago* (stage name) from the inn at which they or their predecessors used to stay.

A Female Society

In the past, most of the maiko and geiko in Gion were from the area and its vicinity. There were many "geiko families" in which the grandmother, the mother and the daughters all entered the profession, the intricacies of which were handed down from generation to generation. In many cases daughters of the okiyas and ochayas became maiko and geiko while their mothers were still working there. Though the number of women in the profession has declined considerably, the fundamental geiko family structure still exists.

The geiko cannot marry if she is to remain in the profession. Even if she has a *danna* (patron) she is still legally single and if she has a child, it is considered illegitimate. A danna usually has to be a man with a respected and powerful position to maintain a geiko and does not want his patronage made public. Therefore many of these men do not recognize the children they have with geiko. Some, however, may visit their child occasionally.

Historically, Japanese wives felt that affairs with the geiko were preferable to those with other women: a wife did not usually feel threatened by such relationships as the geiko's services were of a professional nature and would not disrupt her marriage. Indeed in some instances the family of a regular customer would keep in close contact with the geiko.

In the past there has been a preference among the Japanese for their children to be male – women who gave birth to girls caused disappointment to their family. In the hanamachis, the exact opposite was – and still is – true and boys here are likely to have a difficult time. Around the age of fifteen, they probably have to leave home unless they become an *otokosu* (kimono dresser), which is the only male profession in the community. If a boy does not leave the hanamachi at an appropriate age, he may become a target for gossip and rivalry among the male customers, who may speculate on his relationship with the women. Boys used to be sent to relatives, foster parents, or into apprenticeships but nowadays many prefer to go away to school, before going to university or finding a job.

A Gion inhabitant recalls that before World War Two, girls considerably outnumbered boys at local primary schools and most became maiko and then geiko, like their mothers. Towards the end of their primary education, they attended Yasaka Nyokoba Gakuen, an establishment where maiko and geiko were trained. Since the introduction of child protection laws after the war, a prospective maiko must remain at school until she is fifteen before she start her apprenticeship in the okiya as a *minarai-san* (apprentice maiko).

Opposite: A maiko and a geiko sit in front of the traditional tokonoma alcove in a Kamishichiken teahouse.

Below: In a Ponto-cho teahouse the *okasan* (mother of the okiya) makes arrangements with one of her geiko.

A hanamachi family (from the left): a geiko, an okasan, an ookii-(senior) okasan and a maiko.

Among maiko applicants are a few who have moved to Kyoto to finish their education, lodging in an okiya. Leaving their parents' house to live among strangers can be hard on girls of such a young age, as they are expected to do their share of household chores and run errands to earn their keep. But living in a hanamachi and observing the manners, customs and practices that are involved gives them an early insight into the requirements of their calling. Furthermore, becoming acquainted with the inhabitants of the hanamachi at a young age is a distinct advantage.

Personal relationships are an vital element of life in Kyoto's hanamachis. To be successful, the young maiko must be liked and valued by the *onesans* – the geikos of the house who take the role of elder sisters – and the *okasans* – managers of the teahouses who also act as mother figures within the hanamachi hierarchy. If she is liked, they take good care of her, advising her and helping her with any problems that may arise, and taking her to their ozashikis and other engagements to introduce her to their customers. The importance of these relationships cannot be stressed too highly. It is no exaggeration to say that a maiko who does not form them is unlikely to succeed as a geiko, whatever her artistic talents and charms.

The Hanamachi Family

The okiya is where the okasan, apprentice maiko, maiko, and geiko who have not yet become independent live together. In Kyoto, the okiya is also called *yakata*, meaning residence. Frequently, an okasan is not only the manager but also the owner of the okiya. An okasan is usually a former geiko or the daughter of one of the inhabitants of the okiya who has succeeded her mother.

An okiya accommodates three or four maiko and a similar number of geiko. Echoing the family structure, the women live like sisters, sharing rooms that are used as living quarters by day and where they sleep on futons at night. Their walls are adorned with dolls, postcards from friends and photos taken at the banquets. In addition to the shared living quarters is a separate room for the okasan, another room for making up and getting dressed, a dining room and a kitchen. Only women are allowed to enter the okiya.

The okasan cares for the maiko and geiko exactly as if they were her own daughters. This relationship between the women continues throughout their life in the hanamachi. Nowadays, maiko and geiko enter the profession as a matter of choice, but once it was not uncommon for girls to be exchanged by their poverty-stricken parents for money. In such circumstances it is understandable that the women craved a familial structure, even if it was not their real one. Various traditional ceremonies and customs of the hanamachi can be interpreted as the manifestation of efforts made to forge the ties of respect, affection and obligation that are found in an ordinary family. One geiko told me that these family ties are often so strong, they seem to carry the hanamachis' very history.

The styles of address in the hanamachi are not based on age, as is usual in Japanese families, but seniority. The manager of the okiya or ochaya is always referred to as okasan irrespective of her age. A geiko is always addressed as onesan – even if she is elderly. As for the sisters, those who acquire maiko or geiko status have seniority over those who have not and must be addressed as onesan even if they are younger. This structure must be strictly observed – it is pointless arguing with an okasan even if she is wrong; maiko and geiko must obey her and their senior onesans.

A willingness to learn and respect rules and procedures as well as customs and practices is a basic commitment that the maiko and the geiko must make in order to live and work in a hanamachi. It is equal in importance to their artistic training. Some geiko have told me that it is much more difficult in the early stages of training to learn the rules and manners of their hanamachi than to learn the dances or how to play the musical instruments. Greetings and civilities are part of these complex matters, not only those extended to the customers, but to everyone within the ochayas and the okiyas. When geiko and maiko meet in the street, at school or at a banquet, the less senior must always offer the first greeting, distinctly and clearly. With some exceptions, customers are usually addressed as *oniisan* meaning elder brother, irrespective of their age. However, textile merchants from areas such as Nishijin and owners of restaurants are called *otosan* (father), even if they are young. At a banquet sponsored by a company, a customer is referred to as *shacho-san* or, in abridged form, *shassan*, meaning company president – it does not matter whether he is actually a president or not. Such forms of address are designed to flatter as well as acknowledge respect for seniority and are an important element of hanamachi hospitality.

According to one senior geiko, however, some of the rules governing seniority are becoming less strict. Formerly, for example, a junior geiko would be expected to wash an elder sister's back and arrange her cosmetics on the dressing table. Nowadays it is almost impossible to expect a maiko to do such things. Despite their traditions, the hanamachis are not necessarily an exception to the social changes in Japan, which has seen a decline in the observance of etiquette in recent years.

An okasan welcomes guests at a Gion teahouse.

The okasans of both ochaya and okiya keep a close eye on a maiko throughout her training and their responsibilities often overlap. They teach her how to behave in all circumstances, and their advice may cover such details as the kind of kimono to wear on which occasion (for example, on a visit to her home town, for duty at the ochaya or for an outing with a customer). The okasan of the okiya takes care of the maiko's daily life, paying all her expenses for board and lodging, providing pocket money, buying kimonos, arranging hairdressing, tuition – even her personal effects. The okasan of an ochaya is in charge of all matters relating to banquets, including the entertainments that the maiko and geiko will provide. The ochaya that undertakes the training of the minarai-san is called *minarai-jaya*.

Maiko have no set curriculum in matters of rules and manners – they learn by following and observing the behaviour of their elder sisters. But every day, no matter how late they have been working at an ozashiki the previous evening, they and the geiko have to rise early to go to school. From morning to afternoon, they attend a special school to learn dancing and music and practice the tea ceremony. After lessons, maiko and geiko return to the okiya and do their chores. At about four o'clock, they start making up and getting dressed for a banquet – ozashiki – which usually begins around five-thirty or six. Requests for their presence at an ozashiki, including those for the *jimae* (independent) geiko, always come via the ochaya and are then assigned by the okiya. Even if a maiko has not been engaged she must be ready at her okiya in case her services are suddenly requested.

An okiya is a hive of activity during early-evening preparations. Jimae geiko arrive to get ready with the maiko and geiko who live at the okiya. In Gion, the otokosus come in to help the maiko and geiko put on their kimonos, as do their female counterparts in the other hanamachis. At one time the otokosus were the confidants and advisors of the maiko and geiko but today there are only five left in the profession and they are so busy, going from okiya to okiya, that they no longer have time to fulfil this role.

Usually the okiya family will have tea or a light meal together as maiko and geiko never eat with the customers at the ozashiki. Then they walk or take a taxi to the ochaya or restaurant. If the banquet is not at their usual teahouse, it is customary for the maiko and geiko to drop in there en route, to perform a greeting, although nowadays this is often done over the phone. Once at the teahouse they enter by the private entrance as they are considered family members. They exchange greetings with the okasan, elder geiko and other colleagues who will be present that evening. They also greet the nakais who serve the meals and drinks and the maid who will have just finished preparing the room.

Soon after, dishes for the banquet are delivered by young men from the *shidashi* (a specialist kitchen that caters for ochayas). Ochayas do not have catering facilities, so there are many shidashis in or near the hanamachis. These delivery boys, newsboys and bill collectors are among the few men who are allowed to enter through the ochaya's private entrance.

BELOW: A geiko is assisted as she dons in her kimono ready for a banquet.
OVERLEAF: Maiko and geiko prepare themselves for a banquet.

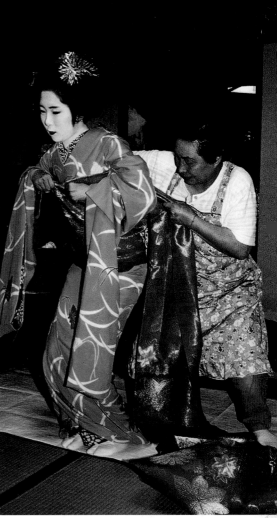

Until the beginning of the 1950s, the maiko had no leisure time. However these days, a maiko is allowed two days a month, which she always anticipates eagerly. On these days she can do as she likes. Her life may look colourful and glamorous, but in reality it is hard and disciplined. Compared with that of her contemporaries, it is also very restricted. Before she does anything she must consult and report to her okasan. She has little time to watch television, she seldom meets members of the opposite sex, other than the customers at a banquet, and when she does see old classmates at a reunion, she is likely to find she no longer has anything in common with them.

Privacy and Price

Rumours have a tendency to spread like wildfire within the hanamachis. Nevertheless, the privacy of customers is paramount and there is no gossip outside the community. Customers are able to enjoy themselves in a relaxed atmosphere, forgetting their daily life. They have confidence in the discretion of the hanamachi. A maiko who abuses a customer's privacy or discloses any details of a banquet is not likely to remain a maiko.

The ozashiki – the word also refers to the room in which the banquet is held – is a private occasion for customers to enjoy the company of maiko and geiko. The unwritten practice of refusing admittance to strangers (ichigen-san okotowari) is based on a belief that their presence would disrupt the atmosphere. Customers will sometimes take photos and give them to a maiko or geiko but an outside photographer would not be welcome at a ozashiki. Customers do not want a permanent record of their activities as the risk of such information emerging in the public domain is too great.

Such secrecy leads to curiosity and questions among those who have never attended a hanamachi banquet. How much does it cost? What is the relationship between a geiko and her danna? How much does a man pay to become a danna? What kind of people are frequent customers? How much do they spend? It is almost impossible to give accurate answers as costs vary on an individual basis. The ochaya has some degree of discretion, taking a customer's ability to pay into account. *Goshugis* (tips) for the maiko and the geiko are either handed to them directly or included in the ochaya's bill, together with the *hanadai* (time charges) for their services. The goshugi must be put in a decorated envelope called a *noshi-bukuro* – money is never proffered uncovered. If the goshugi is given directly to the maiko and geiko, the okasan is notified so that she can also thank the customer.

Goshugis constitute the basic income of the maiko and geiko. Generally, the goshugi from a customer is a minimum of 10,000 yen – a lot of money for the teenaged maiko who, if they worked in a hamburger shop, would earn approximately 800 yen an hour. Some okasans say that the maiko are spoiled. Undoubtedly, their sense of the value of money is quite different from that of other young women of their age. But their income is not consistent – it fluctuates with the economy – and living in the hanamachi is not cheap.

A serene early morning view of an ochaya's banqueting room – a sharp contrast to its appearance the evening before.

Opposite: A geiko and maiko stand in front of an ochaya in Kamishichiken.

Maiko

The kimono of the maiko is quite different from the ordinary Japanese kimono both in appearance and the way in which it is worn. It is vividly coloured and the fabric is very expensive. Worn with a long sash called an *obi* and high-heeled wooden sandals called *okobo*, the sight of a maiko teetering through the historic streets of the hanamachi is one of the enduring images of Kyoto. Tourists come to the city to see its temples and shrines, its gardens and other historic sites, but they also want to see the maiko. And on occasions such as the Gion and Hassaku festivals in which the maiko and their older counterparts participate, tourists and photographers flock to Kyoto to watch them.

A maiko and her onesan in front of her ochaya on the day of the maiko's omisedashi.

Maiko

What are Maiko?

Before World War Two, many maiko came from poor families. Because she provided them with a source of income, she worked very hard to succeed in her hanamachi, from which it was unlikely that she could escape. Today, however, no one becomes a maiko as a result of poverty and a maiko chooses her profession of her own free will.

The motives for wanting to be a maiko vary. Some girls become maiko because they appreciate traditional arts, dance and music, and have taken lessons since they were little. Others become enchanted with the idea after coming to Kyoto on a school outing – the city is a very popular destination for such trips. Some do not want to settle down into married life like their mothers, concentrating on household matters and bringing up children but instead seek a life that they see as a challenge, in which they can develop their individuality. Some want to be maiko for just a few years before they get married although, strictly speaking, someone who sees the role as temporary should not be employed as they are apprentice geiko, not an independent profession. And some, frankly, have stars in their eyes, dreaming of attracting a celebrity or a millionaire and marrying him or hoping that being a maiko will be a stepping stone to fame as a film actress or television star. Once there was a romance between a famous actor and a geiko and, as a result, the number of maiko applicants increased dramatically.

There are still maiko from families that run okiyas or ochayas or who are the daughters of geiko, but the days when recruitment was mostly local and easy are gone. Today, there are only fifty-five maiko in Kyoto and every hanamachi faces a shortage. In Japanese society as a whole, where women have more opportunities than ever before, most young women do not consider the life of a maiko an option – even some hanamachi families advise against it because of the difficulties of the life. In 1982 and 1991, Gion-Higashi and Kamishichiken advertised for maiko in leaflets and magazines. Kamishichiken recruited five maiko this way and three are still active there as geiko. However, advertising as a means of recruitment has not been attempted since then as it was felt to be inappropriate for the hanamachi communities with their strong respect for tradition.

A maiko is recruited through an okiya or ochaya. This is usually done through personal recommendation – a prospective maiko cannot contact the okiya directly, as applicants would normally do with a prospective employer in other professions; someone must make the introductions for them. If an applicant knows no one who can do that, she can get in touch with the okiyas' association, which will arrange an introduction for her.

Two maiko at a Kyoto shrine during the Taisho period (1912–26).

Once an introduction has been made, an applicant visits the okiya with her parents. If both parties agree, the applicant, whether from the Kyoto area or further afield, moves into the okiya as a *shikomi-san*, acting as a maid and observing the maiko and geiko. There is no written contract between the parties, only a verbal agreement in accordance with the traditions and customs of the hanamachis. In some hanamachis, there is no shikomi period, the newcomer immediately becoming minarai-san (apprentice maiko).

Although most trainees now begin their apprenticeship at fifteen, some come into the profession at the age of eighteen after graduating from high school. There are also a few college or university graduates who bypass the position of maiko and make their debut as a geiko after a period of appropriate training, assuming that they can perform to a certain level of artistic accomplishment.

A Maiko's Training

The period of shikomi lasts for about a year, differing slightly between hanamachis. Some quick learners complete their shikomi in as little as eight

LEFT: Dressed in her trailing kimono with her high-waisted obi, a maiko sits in the entrance hall to an Ochaya. RIGHT: A maiko sitting in characteristic pose on tatami mats.

months. While she is a shikomi-san, a girl wears a simple kimono and her hair in a style of her preference, although she must grow it long so that when she becomes a maiko, it can be dressed in the complex and artistic styles that tradition dictates.

For many shikomi-san, the kimono is a new experience. Japanese women now seldom wear kimonos in modern times except on special occasions such as the new year, a wedding or a coming-of-age. But as the kimono is the hallmark of the hanamachis, the shikomi-san must get used to wearing it in her everyday life and practise putting it on correctly and quickly, with all its accessories.

Kimonos are folded in a specific way and kept in a chest of drawers called a *tansu* made from Japanese paulownia wood (they are not kept in a wardrobe or closet as on a hanger they would sag). The maiko must learn how to fold a kimono correctly as part of her training and is often expected to fold her elder sisters' kimonos as well as her own.

It is no longer customary for the Japanese to sit with their feet tucked under their hips – today many houses only have one tatami room or none at all. However, chairs and sofas are not used in the okiya and ochaya. Sitting on the tatami while wearing a kimono is a difficult accomplishment and at first a trainee's feet and legs are likely to become numb after twenty or thirty minutes. Although it is wearing, the young maiko have to be able to sit in this position for several hours when practising the tea ceremony or learning musical instruments.

The life of the shikomi-san is strenuous and her day is long. Everyone in Japan takes a bath before going to bed, but the shikomi-san has to wait until after her elder sisters have theirs when they return from their engagements – often not until the early hours of the morning. It may be three before she gets her turn – and she has to be up again early in the morning if she has to be at school. Between work and school she has little time to herself and she has to review and rehearse what she has learned at school. Most shikomi-san go short of sleep and look forward to the two days off a month to which, like the minarai-san and the maiko, they are entitled. It is with the hope of becoming maiko that the shikomi-san perseveres. However, some inevitably leave the hanamachis without becoming a maiko because they find the life too hard.

The shikomi-san who succeeds in completing this first period of training then becomes a minarai-san for about a month. She adopts *shironuri* – the distinctive white paste make-up that is applied to the face – and wears the trailing kimono known as an *ohikizuri*, which has long full sleeves, together with an obi that is tied with one end hanging. She has to learn how to conduct herself correctly while wearing the ohikizuri, holding up its train as she walks and keeping her back straight at all times so that the obi, which reaches from breast to waist, is kept taut. Carriage and deportment, the way in which to bow correctly as she enters a banquet, dealing with customers and entertaining are all things the minarai-san must learn from her okasans and onesans.

A maiko with her traditional paper umbrella. These are seldom seen anywhere today but in the hanamachis.

THE LANGUAGE OF THE HANAMACHIS

Another skill that the shikomi-san and maiko must master is the hanamachi variant of the Kyoto dialect (*Kyo-kotoba*), which is particularly difficult for anyone not born in the area. Japan has many local dialects, but Kyoto's, believed to have its origins in the Imperial court, is highly individual. It is soft and gentle in tone and is less definite in expression than the norm, a certain vagueness often making it necessary to read between the lines to grasp its nuances. In his masterpiece written at the beginning of the nineteenth century, *Tokaidochu Hizakurige*, a story of two men travelling from Edo (Tokyo) to Osaka, the well-known nineteenth-century novelist Ikku Juppennsha wrote about the tenderness of the Kyoto language compared with that of Edo. At the time, the language, adapted from the Imperial court by merchants' wives, had spread into the various sectors of the community and had sub-divisions according to position and profession, such as nobleman, merchant, craftsman and farmer. That of the hanamachis was yet another division, with its own vocabulary, idiom and accents.

Since the 1960s, largely due to the influence of television, the younger generation in Kyoto has spoken standard Japanese and the verbal distinctions between occupations has disappeared. But Kyo-kotoba continues to be spoken in the hanamachis. The dialect is respected as being as much an identifying feature of the hanamachis as the kimono and its delicacy is regarded as contributing to the womanliness of the maiko and geiko.

San-San-Kudo

The end of the shikomi and minarai training periods is followed by a ceremony called *san-san-kudo* (literally three-times-three exchanges). Originally part of a samurai marriage and still part of the normal Japanese wedding ceremony, in this context the san-san-kudo bonds the new maiko and the geiko who will be her onesan. The pair offer sake to each other, both drinking it in three mouthfuls from three small shallow-bottomed cups.

At the ceremony the maiko is given a new name, usually including one of the characters from her elder sister's. A name such as Katsuno or Katsuma, for example, would relate a maiko to an elder sister called Katsuji – in this way a family of geiko and maiko can be identified.

A new maiko's onesan usually belongs to the same okiya and often to the same minarai-jaya where the apprentice learns her craft. It is the onesan's

A maiko glances in the mirror to check her outfit on the day of her omisedashi.

responsibility to teach her charge all there is to know about life in the hanamachi and to give her advice, even on personal matters. Such an elder sister is both instructor and supervisor and the maiko must respect her and obey her. In return, the onesan will protect the maiko. If there are complaints about her from customers, teachers or colleagues, they will be made to the elder sister, not her – an advantage to the maiko, especially at the beginning of her training as she is protected from direct criticism. A maiko's elder sister may even offer apologies on her behalf.

A senior geiko can have dozens of younger sisters, both maiko and geiko,

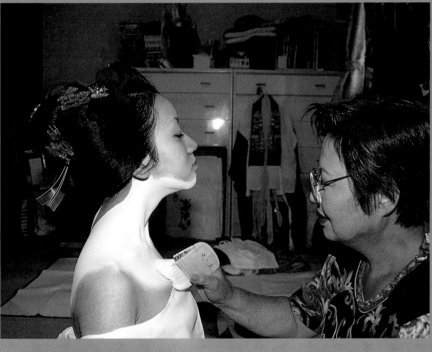

A maiko is prepared for her debut. Ordinarily a maiko will apply her make up herself, but on this day a make-up artist is employed. Three lines, rather than the usual two, are left unpainted on the back of her neck.

and her younger sisters in turn have their own young sisters. The number of sisters a geiko has is a measure of her status and popularity. Despite the importance of these relationships, some maiko today do not have an elder sister. Such a maiko keeps her own name, un-related to others. Being outside the system gives her more independence – but she cannot expect the protection that is inherent in belonging to it.

The san-san-kudo ceremony takes place on a day that is deemed lucky in a fortune-teller's almanac. In Ponto-cho, the venue is the Hanamachi Association Secretariat; in Gion and Miyagawa-cho it takes place in the new maiko's minarai-jaya. Everyone taking part is dressed in a formal black, crested kimono and the seating order is fixed.

The procedures slightly differ from one hanamachi to another. In Ponto-cho, for example, a hanging scroll of Amaterasu-Oomikami (the shinto sun god) is hung on the wall in the tokonoma and a golden folding screen (*kin-byobu*) is placed on either side. The onesan, the new maiko and the okasan of her okiya sit on the left facing the alcove, while on the right sit the eldest geiko from the maiko's minarai-jaya representing its other members: a senior geiko (*ookii-onesan*) who is the elder sister of the new maiko's elder sister, and the minarai-jaya's okasan. The presidents of the teahouse association and the geiko association act as witnesses.

Once the exchange of sake between the new maiko and her elder sister

A maiko dressed in a black, crested ceremonial kimono on the day of her omisedashi.

LEFT: **There is only one *mokuroku* painter left in Kyoto, here he paints a mokuroku for a maiko's debut.**
RIGHT: **A *tenugui* (hand towel) bearing the names of a maiko and her onesan. Such towels are given out as greetings by the maiko and geiko.**

has been completed, the ceremony continues with the maiko exchanging cups with the okasan of the ochaya and then with the remaining five principals.

San-san-kudo, which signals the formal acceptance the new maiko into the hanamachi family, is one of the most important and solemn ceremonies in a maiko and geiko's life and it is not unusual for the maiko and her okasans to be moved to tears.

Debut of a Maiko

On the day after the san-san-kudo, another ceremony called *omisedashi* takes place, celebrating the maiko's debut. Pieces of rectangular paper called *sashigami*, with the names of the new maiko, her elder sister and their okiya are distributed to okiyas, ochayas, restaurants and other establishments in the hanamachi. Owners of the hanamachi shops that sell kimonos, accessories and other goods bring goshugis put inside noshi-bokuros, and the Japanese custom of distributing hand towels on special occasions is followed, these are inscribed in red with the names of the maiko and her elder sister, together with the character *kotobuki*, which symbolizes happiness.

In Ponto-cho, the onesan or a make-up artist will apply the maiko's make-up. The ookii-onesan and the other sisters of the minarai-jaya, all wearing the plain-coloured kimonos that are worn on semi-formal occasions, help her dress and prepare herself. The maiko wears the *ware-shinobu*, the first hairstyle of

FLOWER CHARGES

A banquet in the hanamachi is expensive, but its costs are difficult to calculate and almost impossible to explain to outsiders. These charges include the *hanadai* – usually called *ohana* in the community – which are the charges (literally, flower charges) for the services of the maiko and geiko. The charges are the same for both the maiko and the geiko.

Before clocks were common, the time charge was calculated by *osenko* (incense stick). If one stick was burned, the charge was counted as *ippon* (one unit). The length of ippon differed according to the length of the stick used. Nowadays, twelve units equal an hour in Gion, whereas four units equal an hour in Ponto-cho.

The hanadai is imposed on a customer not only during a banquet but on other occasions, when, for example, he invites the maiko or geiko for *gohan-tabe* (a meal). He pays this charge in addition to paying for lunch or dinner and transport. The same applies when he takes a maiko or geiko to a kabuki performance or on an outing. Occasionally maiko and geiko travel to a banquet, party or event in such places as Tokyo. Again, the hanadai is applied for all the hours spent outside the hanamachi. The units mount rapidly.

There is also the system of called *oasobi* (literally, fun or amusement) under which a customer can buy a number of units of hanadai for his favourite, so that she can have time off to spend as she wishes, not necessarily in his company. Formerly, there were other systems, *soji-nuke* and *omatsuri-nuke* (*soji* means sweeping, *omatsuri* festival, and *nuke* escape). Maiko and geiko were usually very busy on an annual soji day and on the days of omatsuri, but by paying the time charge, a customer or a danna could set the maiko or geiko free from their obligations.

In Gion-Kobu, when the new maiko has sold a thousand units, she celebrates *senju-iwai* (a thousand fortune ceremony). This celebration is very informal. A pair of dumplings in red and white or in steamed rice with red beans, is distributed to the ochayas, okiyas, restaurants and shops in the hanamachi together with *noshi-gami* – a specially designed document – that announces her success.

Maiko and geiko receive the time charges. But maiko may not know exactly exactly how much their hanadai is – a hangover, perhaps, from the days when they were expected to be beautiful dolls and should know little of the outside world and matters of business.

---

her maiko career, with three pieces of red and silver *miokuri* paper on both sides of her chignon, together with a special ornamental tortoise-shell *kanzashi* (hair decoration). Her white-painted make-up leaves three lines unpainted at the back of her neck, instead of the usual two.

The maiko's hairstyle is very delicate and complex and therefore time-consuming and expensive. A maiko usually visits a hairdresser once a week and takes care not to spoil her hairstyle in bed, sleeping uncomfortably with an *omaku* (a high lacquer-painted wooden box topped by a small cushion) behind her neck. Only when her apprenticeship is over and she becomes a geiko is she able, initially, to wear a *katsura* (wig) instead.

The okiya is always busy when making preparations for omisedashi. It prepares a set of kimonos for the new maiko (including one for each of the four seasons) underwear, ornaments, accessories and small articles such as *tabi* (socks), a hand mirror, and an *ozashiki-kago*, which is the small basket handbag that maiko and geiko use for banquets. If everything were to be bought new, it is estimated that the cost of kitting out a maiko would be around ten million yen. There is a popular saying in Japan that the people of Kyoto are as extravagant in dress as those of Osaka are in food. A maiko's costume is expected to be stunning, which is why the goshugi are expected to be lavish – thrift is not part of the hanamachi way of life, especially on an occasion such as this.

The front of the minarai-jaya and the ground floor are hung with *mokuroku*, colourful posters that usually measure 110 by 80 centimetres and bear symbols representing happiness and good fortune (for example Ebisu, the Shinto god of wealth, the crane and tortoise which are symbols of long life, the *takarabune*, a treasure boat, or perhaps male and female masks called *hyottoko* and *okame*). Brief congratulatory phrases such as "Happy Day" or "For Great Prosperity" are written with brushes using black ink and other colouring materials dissolved in water or glue to allow shading. Before World War Two, mokurokus were even larger (160 by 100 centimetres) and more elaborate and many more of them were seen. Today, however, there is only one mokuroku painter left in all Kyoto's hanamachis.

The mokurokus are presented to the new maiko by her elder sister, other geiko and colleagues and sometimes by kabuki and movie actors who are onesan's regular customers. Friends from other hanamachis also send her smaller mokurokus. The okasan often prepares a tier of food boxes which includes dishes especially prepared for the day (sea bream grilled with salt and steamed rice with red beans, or sushi) and has it delivered to maiko at the minarai-jaya.

On the morning of omisedashi day, the new maiko puts on new okobo and visits the ochayas and restaurants where banquets are held to exchange greetings. Her onesan accompanies her, other than in Gion where she is accompanied by an otokosu instead. Dozens of amateur photographers from near and far wait for hours in front of the teahouse where the omisedashi takes place to see the new maiko. Sometimes television cameras and magazine reporters turn up. Many ceremonies in the hanamachis are restricted, as they do not like to draw too much public attention to themselves, but this is different.

For the three days after the omisedashi, the new maiko wears a black, crested kimono and for the following three days, a coloured, crested kimono. On all these days she is taken every evening by her onesan to her banquets and introduced to the customers. The customers give the new maiko generous goshugis – a minimum of 10,000 yen.

Immediately after her debut, the new maiko is likely to be too exhausted to attend any engagements. For many maiko their debut passes in a blur and certainly for a short time a new maiko feels overawed by the experienced way in which senior geiko entertain and make conversation. As time passes, however, she gains confidence, becomes acquainted with more customers – she is engaged for more and more banquets and is finally ready to become a geiko.

Smiling, a maiko is congratulated on the day of her omisedashi.

The Life of a Geiko

Whereas the word "maiko" means a woman of dancing (*mai*), "geiko" means a woman of art (*gei*). The maiko, with her bright trailing kimono, ornate hairstyles and ornamental kanzashis, cannot help but catch the eye. The geiko, however, who dresses much less elaborately, must attract attention through her accomplishments, the intelligence of her discourse, her personality and her behaviour.

In the month before becoming a geiko, a maiko wears the *sakko* hairstyle, the last of five hairstyles worn during her apprenticeship.

The Life of a Geiko

When a maiko first becomes a geiko, she continues to wear a trailed kimono and white make-up, although she covers her hair in a katsura. Once she reaches her thirties, her mode of dress changes again and she wears an ordinary ankle-length kimono and her hair, whether short or long and tied up, is simply arranged. The senior geiko looks no different than any other Japanese woman in a kimono. Only if she is asked to dance does she wear a trailed kimono, katsura and white make-up.

Erikae

A maiko becomes a geiko at the age of twenty or twenty-one – younger, if the okasan thinks she is sufficiently mature. The transition is recognized by the *erikae* – the change of neck band from the maiko's red to the geiko's white. For a month before the erikae, the maiko wears the *sakko* hairstyle – the last of the five hairstyles of her maiko days – with a tortoiseshell kanzashi. Three lines are left unpainted on her nape as was the case on the day of her omisedashi and is the case whenever formal kimono is worn. Her obi is plain and without the maiko's elaborate *pocchiri* (sash clasp), which is decorated with pearls, coral, jade and diamonds. The plainness of her attire symbolizes her transition from the flamboyant dress of the maiko to the understated dress of the geiko, which features little or no red.

The incipient geiko also stains her teeth black for the sakko period. Black teeth date back twelve hundred years to the Heian Period (794–1185) when they were regarded as the sign of a woman's adulthood. In some regions they also indicated a woman's availability for marriage. Although the fashion was prohibited after the Meiji Restoration (1867), it still continued in a few areas until the Taisho Period (1912–26). Today, only the hanamachis of Kyoto maintain the tradition. The black dye was once concocted by mixing iron, tea leaves, sake, candy and rice gruel. Now it is bought in hanamachi cosmetic stores. Geiko have to be careful not to eat hot or fatty dishes as they cause the dye to fade.

Unlike the san-san-kudo, which heralded the maiko's debut, there is no ceremony for the erikae but, as happened on her omisedashi, hand towels and *noshigami* (painted scrolls) are distributed and the new geiko makes her round of visits in the hanamachi. In Gion she performs a dance called *"Kurokami"* (black hair). For three days after her erikae, the new geiko wears a black, crested kimono and for the three days after that, a coloured, crested one. From the seventh day she dons the geiko's normal attire.

Although the okiya does not have to provide her with all the kimonos and

On the day of her erikae a geiko wears the katsura for the first time – she is helped by a hairdresser, but thereafter must put it on by herself.

OPPOSITE: The back view of a geiko: she is wearing the *kuro-montsuki* – formal black kimono with crests.

MIZUAGE

Up until World War Two, there was a ceremony that marked the process of becoming a geiko. It was called *mizuage*, a word that originally meant the unloading of a ship's cargo or catch of fish and later income from an entertainment business – but which in this context was a euphemism for the maiko's defloration.

If she had a danna, it was he who deflowered her. If not, the task fell to a *mizuage-danna* or *erikae-danna*, a man of distinction, well known in the hanamachi and trusted by the okasan to treat the inexperienced girl considerately. There was no relationship between the mizuage-danna and geiko thereafter. According to a former geiko now in her nineties, the president of a big company was her mizuage-danna when she was fifteen. She recalls that she felt ashamed since the change of her neck band instantly signified that she had lost her virginity.

During the time the mizuage was practised, many women got married in their teens and the ceremony was considered necessary for the geiko's passage into adult womanhood. However, sexual relationships are now a matter for the maiko and geiko alone.

accessories needed for this next stage of her life, as in the case of omisedashi, it is often customary to present or lend some kimonos to the new geiko. If the new geiko already has a patronage arrangement, her danna usually bears a considerable portion of the expense. Nowadays, as the majority of new geiko do not have a danna, her regular customers step into the breach. An estimated five million yen is needed to equip a geiko.

Independence

Generally speaking, the geiko's term of service (*nenki*) at the okiya is five to six years, including her time as a shikomi-san and then as a maiko. During this period she lives and works there to replay the okiya's expenditure on her behalf. Some who have completed their service before the erikae can leave immediately after it and become jimae – independent. Most still have time to serve – rather more in the case of those who have been elevated to geiko status at an early age.

Every hanamachi has a *geiko-kumiai* (geiko association) which is composed of geiko – with an elderly geiko who is universally trusted and respected as its chairwoman – and which can quickly sort out common day-to-day problems.

After she becomes independent, a geiko takes responsibility for her own life and starts to work as a freelance professional. She moves to her own apartment and now has to arrange her own meals unlike in her maiko days. She continues to take lessons to improve her artistic skills – which is obligatory throughout her career – however, she certainly has more freedom and flexibility than she had in her time in the okiya. She is no longer under the surveillance of the okasan. She can take more time off than the maiko and does not have to stand by in the okiya fully attired when she has no

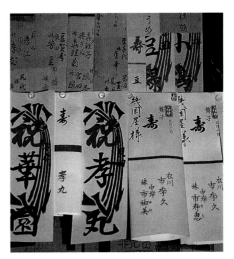

Noshi-gamis that have been presented by geiko and maiko are displayed in a store in a hanamachi.

A geiko dressed and ready for a banquet.

engagements. She is also able to decline a request to attend a banquet. once she is independent. However, a geiko knows it is prudent not to disappoint her regular customers and so is unlikely to decline a request for an engagement. The more popular she becomes, the busier her schedule will be – some geiko are booked up for more than six months in advance. The more banqueting engagements she attends, the more money she earns – although she needs to be talented, and perhaps lucky, to attract rich customers. A geiko can supplement her income substantially by giving performances both in and out of the hanamachi. Geiko who specialize in the shamisen are in particular demand.

Every geiko has large expenses and at the beginning of her career, she is unlikely to have more than a minimum set of kimonos, probably presented by or borrowed from the okiya. She has to acquire more – kimonos, after all, are her stock-in-trade – and they cost a great deal. So do the accessories and ornaments that go with them. Rents in or near the hanamachi are high, and there are other expenses, not least helping her younger sisters to whose ceremonies such as their omisedashis she contributes. A few geiko do not earn enough to maintain themselves and have to leave the profession, but many make a very comfortable living.

Wearing a stunning blue kimono, this geiko sits at the entrance of an ochaya.

ORIGIN OF THE GEISHA

The geisha, who are the counterparts of Kyoto's geiko elsewhere in Japan, can be traced back to the *shirabyoshis*, female courtesans who took their name from the dance they performed. They became popular late in the Heian Period (794–1185 AD) and reached the height of their popularity in the Chu-Sei era (twelfth–sixteenth century). The ballads that the shirabyoshis recited were based on a Buddhist prayers introduced from China. The dances they performed were also performed by high court officials, priests and pages and had considerable influence on the style of dancing in the Kin-sei era (seventeenth–nineteenth centuries).

The stories of several shirabyoshis are well known to the Japanese. One is of Gi-oh and her sister Gi-Jo, both mistresses of Premier Kiyomori Taira (1118–81). The Gi-oh temple in Kyoto where Gi-oh spent her life after losing Kiyomori Taira's patronage and where she is buried with her sister and mother, is a very popular tourist spot, especially when the leaves turn in autumn. Another well-known story is of the love of the former shirabyoshi Shizuka-gozen and Yoshitsune Minamoto, younger brother of Shogun Yoritomo Minamato.

It was during the Genroku Era (1688–1704) that the word "geisha" first appeared in Edo (now Tokyo). The geisha was originally called geigi, from the same Japanese character as geiko. The Genroku was an era of peace and stability after Japan adopted a closed-door policy towards other countries. Towns and cities developed and *chonin bunka* (townsmen's culture) flourished. Not having the power to oppose the feudal rulers or to go into politics, townsmen simply pursued day-to-day pleasure – and the hanamachis prospered. It was also during this era that kabuki plays became popular.

In the Horeki Era (1751–64), *taiko-joro*, female Japanese drum players, appeared to supplement the female entertainers, and the *otoko-geisha* (male geisha) who guided the guests in the hanamachis, became an independent profession; called *hokans* (comedians) or *taiko-mochis* (drum bearers). They entertained at banquets in the ochayas, their mimicry and impersonation often impromptu. A famous hokan was Ginko Sakurakawa who was active in Yoshiwara, the most well-known hanamachi in Tokyo during the Edo Period (1603–1853).

Here, top-class geishas were called *oiran* and were the equivalent of Shimabara's tayu in Kyoto. They wore extravagant dresses, tied their obi at the front and put on sandals. They walked in a unique manner called *hachimonji*, drawing an arc with both feet. When they went to a banquet, they were accompanied by many followers including six-to-ten-year-old girls called *kamuro*, as well as by young men. This *oiran-dochu* (parade) is often seen in theatres and festivals.

Oirans are often heroines in kabuki plays. In *Kagotsurube Sato-no-Eizame* by Shinshichi Kawatake III (1842–1901) a man comes to Edo on business and falls in love with an oiran named Yatushashi. He spends a great deal of money to possess her but, discovering that she has a secret lover, he kills her with a sword. A famous writer of kabuki plays, Monzaemon Chikamatsu (1653–1724), also wrote stories featuring oirans. In one, "Meido-no-Hikyaku", a man loses his head over Umekawa and redeems her by robbing his friend and a customer, only to be arrested when he tries to run away with her. Generally speaking, a love story that features an oiran has an unhappy ending.

Once, there were very young female entertainers called *hangyoku* in Tokyo and elsewhere who started their apprenticeship in a hanamachi at the age of nine or ten and appeared at banquets several years later. They danced and played the taiko. They did not wear the kimono with a long train like the maiko, but did wear the distinguishing red neck band. The *gyoku-dai* (time charge) for the hangyoku was half that of a geisha – "han" means half. However, with the introduction of a child protection law that forbade girls under fifteen from working, the hangyoku ceased to exist.

ABOVE: **Geiko in Kyoto: the subdued colour of their kimonos and hairstyles that are less flamboyant than the maiko, indicate their maturity.**

Danna

Once, almost all geiko had a danna. Today, according to one okasan, only about one in five have a patron, although other estimates are higher. The word "danna" actually translates as husband, but in this context it means financial patron. A danna has to be affluent, well acquainted with the hanamachi involved, and a regular customer. In principle, a man can have only one favourite ochaya in any one hanamachi, so that he has the confidence of its okasan. Once, when textiles were one of Kyoto's major industries, many dannas were the owners of the weaving factories in Nishijin. Nowadays, most are company owners and businessmen.

A prospective danna has to follow certain procedures. First he consults with the okasan of the ochaya who ascertains whether or not the geiko is willing to partner him. If she is, the okasan informs her counterpart at the okiya who must also satisfy herself about the geiko's willingness. After this, the two okasans discuss the patronage arrangements with the prospective danna, including the level of financial assistance he proposes to give.

OPPOSITE: **On the day of her erikae a new geiko is guided to the ochayas of Gion by an otokusu.**

Should the geiko find it difficult to refuse the prospective danna's offer out of a sense of obligation to the okasan, she will confide in her onesan who will talk with the two mother figures. The geiko and the prospective danna never discuss the matter directly, which allows either to withdraw from the negotiation without feelings being hurt. – this is characteristic of the way relationships are conducted in the hanamachis. Assuming the patronage is agreed, its terms are not confirmed in writing. While the custom of verbal agreement is not uncommon elsewhere in Japan, it is an unwritten rule in the hanamachis – you do not make an arrangement with a man who cannot be trusted without a piece of paper. There is no ceremony to celebrate the geiko–danna arrangement.

The danna then pays the geiko a monthly allowance, which usually covers the geiko's rent and living expenses; he may also buy her kimonos and obis. In addition he distributes tickets for her artistic performances to his friends and acquaintances. Sometimes he may take her as far afield as Tokyo to see a kabuki play. Regardless of all this, when he asks her to attend a banquet, the danna has to pay the hanadai like everyone else.

The danna's demands on a geiko's time are her first priority. She cannot make an appointment with another man outside the engagement hours and if a customer invites her on an outing with other geiko, she has to ask her patron's permission. Sometimes, however, a patron will pay the geiko's hanadai to let her free to meet someone else. Since a patron is generally much older – in some cases old enough to be a geiko's father – he may be generous in such a matter. In return, the geiko is expected to report every intimate detail of her life to him and it is sensible for her to do so. The information network inside the hanamachi is so close and intricate that it is virtually impossible to keep a secret and if a patron hears something significant about his geiko that she has not revealed, she may lose his trust and his patronage – which has no legal basis.

More often than not, a danna is not only much older than his geiko, but also married. However, there are cases of dannas who are bachelors and who marry their geiko. If this happens and her nenki still has time to run, he has to take over all her outstanding debts to the okiya. He may, of course, wait until the end of her service period, in the meantime continuing to pay her hanadai in order to meet her. Occasionally, when a patron wishes to marry a geiko but is reluctant to do so while she belongs to the profession, the okasan will arrange for her to be adopted by a family outside the hanamachi.

If a patron wishes to break off his relationship with a geiko, he consults the okasans of both okiya and ochaya. This process is called the *mazu*, which refers to the one-off payment he must make to the geiko. The original meaning of the word is not clear. The okasans discuss with the danna the amount of the mazu, which the geiko receives through them. In addition, the danna must pay the geiko's monthly allowance for three months thereafter. In a case where the geiko wishes to break off the relationship – *hima-wo-morau* – she also consults her okasans. Usually they will try to persuade her not to take this course of action, but if her mind is made up, they will inform the danna. If discontinuing

OPPOSITE: A geiko wearing a formal black kimono.

A geiko sitting in the corridor of a Kamishichiken ochaya.

patronage is the geiko's idea, the danna does not have to pay mazu.

As a result of big economic and social changes in Japan since World War Two, fewer men are rich enough to become a geiko's patron – and some dannas have had to renounce their patronage purely on financial grounds. The decline in the number of dannas is also a result of the fast pace and complexity of modern-day life. Many modern Japanese men who may once have been interested in becoming a danna cannot be now be bothered with the complicated procedures and traditions involved. Japan has also experienced a big decline in interest in the traditional arts. Once, dannas were men well versed in these and they spent a considerable amount of time and money exchanging their knowledge with the geiko, educating her with tender care so that she became the male ideal of accomplished and talented womanhood. Doing this not only contributed to their pleasure but to their standing in society. Today, traditional dance and music are not popular and few men are able to recite traditional ballads and play traditional instruments.

Up to the beginning of the Showa Period (1926–89) most Japanese marriages were arranged by parents and it was difficult for young men from the middle and upper classes to meet women. In such circumstances the world of the geiko and maiko held considerable attraction. Today, however, there are so many opportunities for young men and women to meet that the hanamachis are somewhat redundant and young men are sceptical about a system that charges for the company of a female who cannot be dated directly. The geiko is still regarded as much more than an entertainer – she is an artist who is a precious element of Japan's cultural heritage – but there are many hostesses in high-class clubs and bars where the formalities of the hanamachis do not apply.

The triangle of paper given away at the ceremony of hiki-iwai – it bears the characters of the woman's geiko and real names.

Hiki-iwai

The geiko who starts her career as a maiko with the san-san-kudo ceremony, ends it with the a celebration of retirement called *hiki-iwai*. Originally the hiki-iwai marked the completion of a geiko's term of service in the okiya or when she retired from the hanamachi because she has had her debts paid for by her patron. Now it is the occasion on which she announces her retirement and thanks all those who have helped and looked after her during her career. Some geiko – and maiko – feel no sense of indebtedness or obligation to the hanamachi and leave without a hiki-iwai, a matter of regret to the okasans who have taken care of them since they were young. The generation gap is to blame, the okasans believe, and cannot be helped.

If she has talent and personality a geiko can continue to be popular and have regular customers until she is elderly as there is no retirement age, but she may give up at any time for different reasons. She may be opening a restaurant, bar or other business in or out of the hanamachi, she may be marrying her lover or she may simply feel she is too old.

At her hiki-iwai, the geiko makes a gift of rice-boxes to her teachers, okasans, onesans and other colleagues, to express her gratitude. These are delivered with a triangular paper displaying the character for hiki-iwai as well as her geiko and real names. Rice plays a significant role in Japanese culture – rice and rice wine are always dedicated to shrines and temples – and the geiko's career begins as a maiko, and comes to a close, with ceremonies that involve rice.

If the rice in the rice-boxes is white and steamed, it means that the geiko will never return to the hanamachi. If there is some red rice together with red beans called *sasage*, she leaves open the possibility that she will. Prewar, some geiko retired having been redeemed by dannas they did not love. In such cases the geiko would tacitly make her feelings clear to her close friends by having red rice included in the boxes delivered to them without the knowledge of her danna.

Hiki-iwai is very simple and informal, compared with other ceremonies in the hanamachi. It symbolizes the geiko's move from her colourful life in the hanamachi to the life she will lead as an ordinary woman.

The Maiko and Geiko Look

Historically, the Japanese are a people sensitive to the changes of the seasons, finding delicacy and beauty in the transition from one season to another. For Kyoto's maiko and the geiko it is very important that this awareness of the seasons is apparent in their dress. The kimono has to be co-ordinated with underwear, hairstyle, accessories and footwear so that the effect is realized from head to toe. It is the secret of dressing beautifully.

**In her room in an okiya,
a maiko applies her make up.**

The Maiko and Geiko Look

I n addition to the effect of the seasons, the colours and designs of kimonos and all the accessories vary subtly according to the wearer's age. One can talk about the look of the maiko and geiko in general terms but, in practice, there are complicated and detailed rules that govern the overall effect

Two geiko stroll through the narrow streets of Ponto-cho, they are dressed in the informal yukata.

Kimonos

Kimonos can be made from a variety of materials, however, those of the maiko and geiko are always made from silk – except for the *yukata*, or summer kimono, which is made from thin cotton and worn on informal occasions and at home.

The amount of material required to make a kimono is a *tan*, a traditional Japanese measurement which measures 37 centimetres wide by 12 metres long. The maiko's long-sleeved kimono and the young geiko's long trailed kimono require two tans of material. Ready-made kimonos can be purchased in many Japanese department stores and specialist kimono stores, but those of higher-grade material, such as those the maiko and the geiko wear, have to be ordered. This is not necessarily to ensure a better fit – kimonos come in only one size, irrespective of the height or figure – but to ensure exclusivity. Often a very good quality kimono is handed down from mother to daughter through several generations, similarly an okiya will keep many expensive kimonos and accessories for use through the years by maiko and geiko.

Unlike Western dress, the kimono does not follow the line of the body. The basic shape of the sleeves and the body is rectangular, and it is worn by winding it around the body and tucking both ends together, double-folded, at

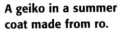

A geiko in a summer coat made from ro.

the front. The right side end must always be folded under the left side – the left end is only ever folded under the right on someone who has died. Kimonos have no buttons or fasteners, but are held together with about twelve braids.

Beneath a kimono, the maiko and geiko wear undergarments called *hada-juban* on the upper body and *naga-juban* which is a full-length. These garments follow the line of the the kimono.

The primary difference between the standard female kimono and those worn by maiko and geiko, is that the latter leaves the nape of the neck uncovered to the shoulders, while with the former, the nape is covered.

Kimono and the Seasons

The material and the lining of kimonos, undergarments and obi are co-ordinated in line with the seasons and sub-seasons, as are the kanzashi and other kinds of accessories the maiko and geiko wear. As many of these involve silk, precious metals and jewels, it is hardly surprising that it costs such a huge amount of money when the maiko and the geiko make their debuts.

Kimonos worn between September and May are double-layered, with a lining cloth called *awase*. The naga-juban are also lined. Like their kimonos, the maiko and geiko's undergarments are made from silk and, as they are often patterned with seasonal flowers, changed according to the time of year. Kimonos worn in December have two layers: another layer called *nimai-gasane* is added to the *awase* and some floss silk is placed between the two at the bottom of the kimono. Such kimonos are made from three tans of material and are extremely heavy to wear.

May and September are the transitional months between the seasons, the naga-juban is worn without a lining cloth but the kimono itself is lined. In June, both the kimono and the undergarments are a single fold without a lining cloth. In July and August, the hottest season in Japan, kimonos are made from *ro*, a thin silk gauze with a very loose weave, and *sha*, coarse woven silk gauze. Kimonos made of ro must have their accompanying undergarments and sashes made from the same material.

Kimono Patterns

In summer the simple, informal cotton yukata is worn, accompanied by simple underwear and without accessories and ornaments. Unlike other kimonos, the style and pattern of a yukata is the same whatever the age of the maiko or geiko. However, the obi and *zori* (sandals) that accompany a yukata become less colourful with age.

Although all other kimonos are made from silk, different ways of weaving the material are employed in their creation, such as the ro and sha already mentioned, *hira-ori* (plain fabrics) and *aya-ori* (twill). The manner of dyeing and processing these materials also varies, and includes, *chirimen* (silk crepe), *shibori* (tie-dyed fabrics) and *habutae* (thick fabrics). Shibori is particularly expensive as it is dyed with spots, fastened by threads and involves considerable time and labour. Various patterns and colours are dyed, in-woven

PREVIOUS PAGES: Detail of the fabric of a maiko's kimono (LEFT) showing motifs of folding fans; there is a seam in the middle, but it is skillfully sewn together so as not to destroy the complex pattern which is drawn and dyed in the Kyo-Yuzen manner. (TOP RIGHT) The fabric used for the maiko's hadajuban underwear and (BOTTOM) for the geiko's.

or embroidered on these materials. *Kyo-yuzen* is an especially well-known dyeing method and carries a high reputation. Yuzen-style dyeing is believed to have been established by Yuzensai Miyazaki, a painter in Kyoto during the Genroku Era (1688–1704) and today there are many kyo-yuzen processing studios in Kyoto. The dyes are made from natural ingredients such as tree bark, flowers, nuts and berries to produce a great variety of colours. Such fabric is very expensive as experienced artists paint the designs and patterns individually; orders for the exclusive material come from all over Japan. Kyo-yuzen is often used to make the geiko and maiko's ceremonial crested kimonos and their *komon-kimono*, which is dyed with fine small patterns. Every summer, newly-dyed kyo-yuzen silk cloth is washed in the Kamo River at the Shijo bridge in an event called *Yuzen-Nagashi*. The sight of the colourful cloths floating on the river is a unique and remarkable spectacle.

Painting Kyo-Yuzen.

The patterns adopted for the hand-painted kyo-yuzen usually follow a classic motif, for example, those seen in the woven fabrics of Tenpyo Era (729–749), or on the copper mirrors presented to the Japanese Emperor by the Tang Dynasty (618–906) of China. These historical designs are safeguarded in the Shosoin, Japan's ancient treasure house in Nara. Other designs originate from Noh and kabuki traditions. These classic patterns, especially those of the Noh plays, are extremely popular among maiko and geiko. So, too, are the traditional Japanese flowers that accompany the seasons: for example, the hydrangea for early summer, morning glory or broad bell flower for mid-summer, Japanese pampas grass for early autumn, scarlet-tinged maple leaves for late autumn, camellia for winter and plum flowers, cherry blossoms or narcissus for spring.

As the material used to make a kimono is only 37 centimetres wide, each garment has many seams, however, it must look as if it were made without any. The immense skill of the kimono makers enables them to cut and sew to adjust the elaborate patterns perfectly – a slippage of only one millimetre would distort the fabric and is not permissible.

Ceremonial Kimonos

In Japan, each family has a family crest called *kamon*, which features on their formal kimonos. Today there are still men and women who wear the crested kimono on formal occasions such as weddings. More than 4,590 different kamons are mentioned in the book called *Monten* – the catalogue of Japanese crests. Each okiya and the ochaya will also have its own "family" crest. A maiko's kimono always bears the crest of her okiya, but the kimono of an independent geiko will bear her own crest. The crests are placed on five different parts of the kimono: on the back, each breast and each sleeve.

The maiko and geiko have two sets of the ceremonial crested kimono one for winter, the other for summer. The New Year and the first week of January is

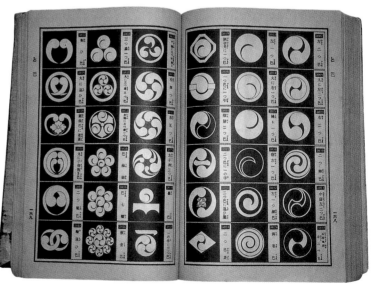

Monten, a catalogue containing more than 4590 Japanese family crests.

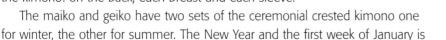

the first of the annual occasions during which the black crested kimono is worn by the young geiko. The patterns on these kimonos are traditionally solemn in keeping with such formal occasions. The maiko's kimono, which is of winter weight, plus all its accessories, weighs almost twenty kilograms, which may be half what she weighs herself, not surprisingly, it takes her some time to get accustomed to it. For the week from January 8, maiko and geiko wear the coloured kimono with crests. The background colour is usually blue or pink – the patterns and colours become more muted according to the wearer's age. The young maiko has patterns on both sides of the shoulders, the senior maiko has patterns on only one side and the geiko has none. The black crested kimono is also worn by the maiko on the occasion of her debut and when she becomes a fully-fledged geiko at the erikae ceremony. On August 1, on the occasion of the *hassaku*, both the maiko and the geiko wear the black crested kimono made from ro. In December, when maikos and geikos attend the Minamiza Theatre for the special kabuki performances given by the all-star casts known as *kaomise*, they wear the coloured, crested kimono.

PREVIOUS PAGES: Fabric for maiko kimonos (LEFT-HAND PAGE, TOP LEFT), the motifs are a mixture of maple leaves, chrysanthemums, wild oranges and plum blossom; (TOP RIGHT) maple leaves; (BOTTOM RIGHT) cherry blossom and (BOTTOM LEFT) a Japanese decorated ball. RIGHT-HAND PAGE: fabric featuring a Chinese phoenix, plum blossom and maple leaves.

OPPOSITE: A crested black kimono for the Erikae ceremony of Mamegiku in Gion Kobu.

BELOW: The maiko's distinguishing red neckband.

DISTINGUISHING GEIKO FROM MAIKO

Unaccustomed to the rules and practices of wearing traditional dress, the younger generation in Japan is probably unaware of the differences in the attire of maiko and geiko.

The **Obi** (sash) is the most obvious distinction between the maiko and geiko. The maiko's obi dangles to her ankles and is unique to her; the geiko's ordinary obi is tied square at her back. The maiko's obi is co-ordinated with a wide and colourful *obi-jime* (sash band) and pocchiri (sash clasp) decorated with such jewels as jade, coral, pearl and diamond. The geiko's sash band, on the other hand, is narrow and her sash clasp is smaller and less ostentatious.

Kimono: The maiko's kimono has long swinging sleeves. The sleeves and shoulders are tucked up, as they are on a child's kimono, which can be let out as the child grows, this harks back to the past when maiko could have been as young as ten years old. The maiko's neck band is usually red. When a maiko wears a long trailed kimono, her long naga-juban undergarment, which hangs below the hem, is also red, while a geiko's is pink. Kimono designs differ according to status and age. The young maiko's has patterns on both shoulders, a senior maiko has patterns on one and a geiko has none. Kimono colours for the elderly geiko are often beige, grey or dark blue.

Hair and make-up: The maiko styles her own hair and always wears white-painted make-up, however, a geiko only wears white make-up in conjunction with the katsura. Usually the geiko does not wear the distinctive white make-up and her hair is either cut short or, if worn long, pinned up like that of ordinary women's.

Kanzashi: A maiko wears many kanzashis (hair decorations) in her hair. The principal one, the *daikan*, is placed at the front of her chignon and changes each month. The geiko's kanzashis are basically of two types: an ivory comb and a hairpin with jade bead for summer (June–September), and a tortoiseshell comb and a hair-pin with coral bead for winter (October–May).

Hakimono (footwear): The maiko wears wooden sandals which stand approximately 10 centimetres high called *okobo*, while the geiko wears wooden clogs called *geta* or leather sandals called *zori*. You can tell how many maiko and geiko are in an ochaya by the number of footwear at the entrance

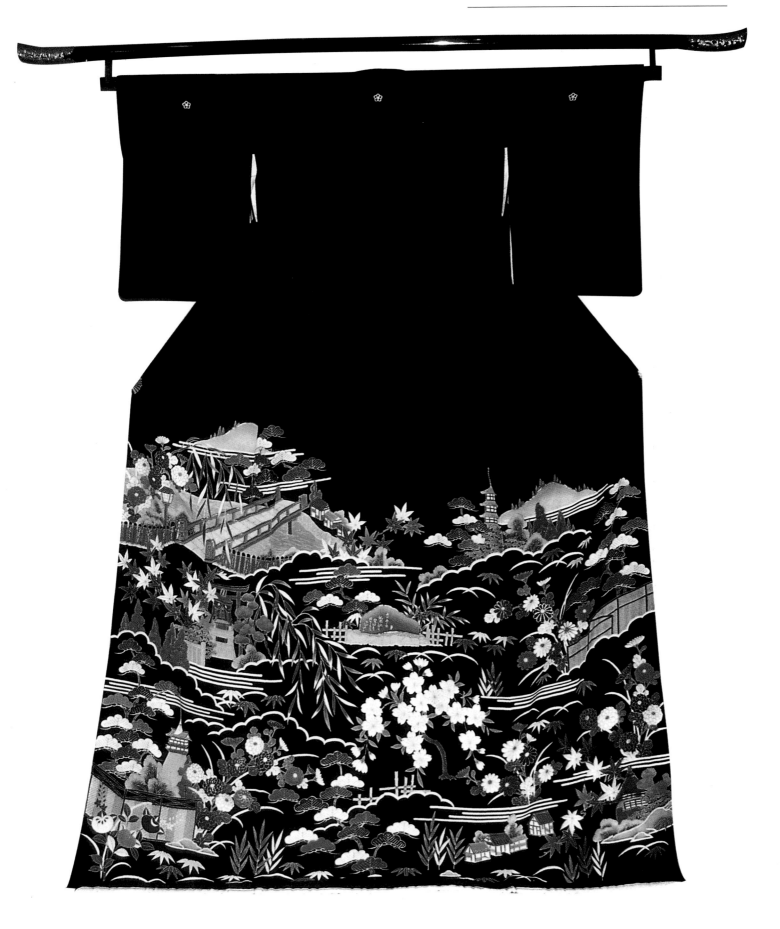

A kimono in a solid colour without any patterns is called *iromuji* it is worn on semi-formal occasions. These kimonos are usually light blue, grey, pink, yellow or ivory in colour. On the occasions when the maiko and geiko go out for a meal or to a theatrical performance with a customer, they wear their fine-patterned komon-kimono. The background colours of these are yellow, pink, or blue for the maiko as they are also for the geiko, although in more subdued shades, the komon-kimono for the elderly geiko are grey or brown.

Other Elements of Dress

Coats or over-garments: When travelling or going out, maikos and geikos always wear a coat or an overgarment to keep their precious kimonos clean. These are ankle-length and always made of silk. In summer, the silk used for coats is ro or sha.

ABOVE, LEFT: Three maiko obis, each of a traditional design. ABOVE, RIGHT: Detail of the obi designed to be worn with the black kimono shown on page 67.

Obis: The obi of a kimono is also made of silk, usually Nishijin fabric, which is regarded as the best in Japan. This style of fabrics originated at the beginning of the Heian Period (794–1185) when the cloth was first woven for the Imperial Court. A maiko's obi, woven with gold and silver threads, is more than 5 metres long and is worn loosely with its end dangling, displaying the crest of her okiya. A hand-woven obi of the highest quality can cost five to six million yen. The geiko's obi, which is called *maru-obi*, is a one-piece sash, 4 metres in length and a little less than 70 centimetres wide. It is double-folded, padded and tied square at the back. Maiko may also wear maru-obi with their komon or iromuji kimonos.

Obi-jime: This is the silk-thread braid that ties on the middle of the obi. This type of braid is said to have come to Japan with the arrival of Buddhism from China in *ad*538. These braids cam be seen today decorating altars and hanging screens in Buddhist temples. The width of the maiko's obi-jime is *issun* (3.3 centimetres), another traditional Japanese measurement. It is woven with various coloured threads, such as red, green, pink, yellow, gold and silver. The geiko's obi-jime is narrower and like the rest of her attire, less colourful.

Brightly coloured maiko obi-jimes (sash bands).

A maiko's pocchiri: the elaborate sash clasp resembles a chrysanthemum carved from pink coral, jade and silver; at its centre is a diamond.

Obi-domes: The maiko's *obi-dome* (sash clasp) is called a pocchiri and variously displays coral, amethyst, jade, diamond and agate, set on the delicately designed silver frame. An pocchiri, is fairly heavy and costs from five hundred thousand to several million yen. The geiko's obi-dome is much smaller and simpler and is made of tortoiseshell, coral, and other materials. Some geiko do not wear one at all.

Obi-age: The *obi-age* is a long, narrow string of thin silk cloth, which helps keep the obi in place. In the case of the maiko, it is red with gold and silver coloured patterns and it is visible above the obi. When she wears a crested kimono, her obi-age is also crested. The colour of the obi-age for the geiko is light pink, blue or other light colours and is usually placed inside the obi.

Eris: Seen above the neck of the kimono, the *eri* is a thickly woven long and narrow cloth. The maiko's is red and luxuriously embroidered with gold and silver threads, fairly heavy and often displaying the crest of her okiya. At the erikae ceremony, when the maiko becomes a geiko, the red neck band is changed for white.

Footwear
Tabi are the socks worn with a kimono by both maiko and geiko. The big toe of the tabi, which are made from white cotton, is separated, so that sandals or wooden clogs can be worn easily. The cloth has no elasticity, but tabi are designed to retain their shape, even when not on the foot. In most cases, people buy ready-made tabi, but the maiko and the geiko usually order theirs to ensure a perfect fit – their attire is their trademark.

A maiko's okobo.

Hakimono or footwear varies, like the rest of a geiko or maiko's attire according to the occasion. The maiko's clogs, called okobo, are 10 centimetres high and made of paulownia wood, which is native to Japan. The colour of the clog's thong varies according to her career: red for the initial period, changing to pink and later purple. Some okobos are covered with fine-knitted straw like tatami mats. When the geiko wears the long trailed kimono with the katsura and white make-up, she puts on *geta* (wooden clogs) that are lower than the okobo but also made of paulownia wood.

There are two kinds of both okobo and geta: plain and black lacquered. Black-painted ones are usually worm in summer as sweat might spoil plain wood, while in the other seasons plain ones are more often the rule.

Both maiko and the geiko wear zori, sandals made of patent leather, with yukata, komon or iromuji. This is a contrast with women in general who wear geta with the yukata and zori with the other kimonos, including formal and informal ones.

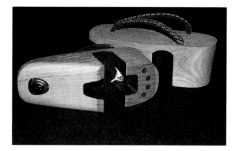

A geiko's geta.

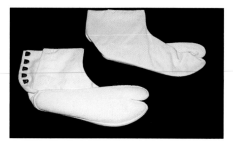

Tabi.

Accessories

Maiko and geiko carry *ozashiki-kago* (a basket-type of handbag with an opening in silk) when they go to banquets. In it they put *nohsatsu* and *senja-fuda* (name cards and stickers bearing the name of their hanamachi), a toothpick case, pocket towels, a folding fan for the dance, absorbent papers, a hand mirror, a *binkaki* (boxwood comb), lip colour, and so on – and, these days, a mobile phone. The maiko's ozashiki-kago is colourful and gaily patterned; the geiko's less flamboyant.

Both umbrellas and parasols – *kasas* – for maiko and geiko are made of bamboo and silk. Such traditional Japanese kasas were formerly used by many families, but nowadays they are rarely seen. In Kyoto, however, some families still include this type of kasa in their daughter's trousseau. The kasa is fairly heavy, but it complements the traditional attire of the maiko and geiko.

A maiko's ozashiki-kago.

Folding fans, used for dancing.

Hairstyles

The traditional Japanese style coiffure worn by the maiko is hardly seen nowadays outside the hanamachis. Until the beginning of the Showa Period (1926–89) the average Japanese woman wore a kimono and had her hair done in the Japanese style either at home or less usually at the hairdresser's. Young girls usually had their hair done by their mother or aunts.

The tension of wearing hair in this traditional fashion for many years often lead to the crown of the head becoming bald, even if it was not detectable and hidden by the rest of the hair. As Japanese women become more Westernized towards the end of the Taisho Period (1912–26) and after it at the beginning of the Showa Period, Japanese-style hair was seen as impractical and began to go out of fashion, like the kimono. Western hairstyles, short or permanently waved, subsequently become popular in big cities.

The number of hairdressers specializing in traditional styles has declined with the decrease of the maiko. Today there are only a few left in the

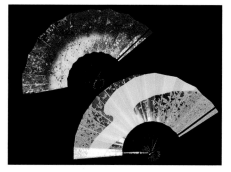

Traditional Japanese parasols.

hanamachis of Kyoto. It takes about forty minutes for the hairdresser to prepare the maiko's hair, and it is very expensive, as a result, she goes to the hairdresser approximately once a week and, like women in former days, sleeps without letting down her hair on an *omaku*, a black-lacquered wooden pillow topped with a small cushion.

At the hairdresser's, the maiko's long hair, which usually reaches down her back, is stretched with tongs. It is then arranged with a special paste pomade called *bintsuke-abura*, which makes the complicated hairstyle last a comparatively long time. (According to the maiko, when they wash their hair, they have to do it several times to remove the pomade.) Japanese hair is thick and heavy compared with Westerners, but the hairdresser may still put a pad of artificial hair called *ketabo* in the side locks, or paper inside the body of the hair, to give it extra shape and support.

There are five basic kinds of maiko hairstyle. The first is called *wareshinobu*, which stresses the maiko's loveliness and is worn in the initial period of her training, including the occasion of her omisedashi. A *kanoko*, a red silk ribbon- with a white spotted pattern, is worn at both the front and the back of the *mage*, the mass of the hair on the crown. For the omisedashi the maiko

The black-lacquered wooden pillow on which a maiko sleeps.

dresses the wareshinobu with special kinds of kanzashis, primarily the silver *bira-kan* (fluttering), *tama-kan* (coral and other beads), *kanoko, kanoko-dome,* and the *miokuri* (three rectangular decorations of red, silver and gold) on the back. When the maiko reaches the age of eighteen or thereabouts, she changes her hairstyle to *ofuku,* where the kanoko is worn only at the back of the mage. In the past the change to this hairstyle would have signified that the maiko had now got a danna.

Katsuyama and *yakko-shimada* are the two kinds of hairstyle that the senior maiko wears on special occasions. The *katsuyama,* named after a top female entertainer in seventeenth-century Edo, is worn for the Gion festival in July. The style has also been called *marumage* and was worn widely by married women until the beginning of the Showa Period. *Yakko-shimada* is worn on formal occasions, such as the New Year celebration, when the maiko's kanzashi are made from dried ears of rice.

For one month proceeding the erikae ceremony for her debut as a geiko, the maiko wears a hairstyle called sakko, for which the top of the piled-up hair is cut. It is said that by having this done, the maiko expresses her resolution and readiness to become a geiko. At this time, the maiko's kanzashis may be tortoiseshell, bira-kan or tamakan, worn together with red-ribbon cloth at the front.

The maiko has other hairstyles for special occasions such as the *Setsubun,* an event that takes place early in February. In Gion-Kobu on the occasion of the *Miyako Odori* (Cherry Dance) the maiko wears the *shimada* wig, which is the same style as the geiko's.

Until the middle 1960s, a geiko dressed her own hair as did the maiko. Gradually the geiko began to wear wigs – katsura. This occurred partly because the number of hairdressers declined and also because the geiko had to change her hairstyle according to the kind of dance she was required to perform at the ozashiki. Another factor in the change was that the technique of making katsuras improved considerably. The wigs used to weigh more than a kilogram; now they are only six hundred grams.

Katsuras are made of human hair that has been washed, cleaned and dyed a natural colour. Every katsura is made individually. The katsura maker measures the geiko's head and visualizes how the wig will best suit her looks and figure. He makes the katsura as if he were a hairdresser, using about ten different-shaped combs. He first dresses the hair with *gindashi-abura,* a kind of gel, and shapes the wig with a paste pomade. As the geiko puts on the wig almost every day, the katsura maker rearranges it twice a month or so, so that it maintains a fresh and glossy appearance. If a katsura is made by a single maker, it would take about two weeks, but nowadays the work is usually done by a small family unit. On average, a katsura costs five hundred thousand yen.

The geiko must have three different katsuras: shimada, *mae-ware,* and *tsubushi-shimada.* The shimada is a formal hairstyle, the tsubushi-shimada is slightly less so. Mae-ware is worn when the geiko plays a male part in a dance performance.

ABOVE AND OPPOSITE: The wareshinobu hairstyle from the front and behind.

The maiko's sakko hairstyle.

Maiko Kanzashis

These hair pins change according to the month and largely depend on what flowers are in bloom at the time; there are also special ones for festivals. The artificial flowers that decorate the kanzashis are always made from silk. Making the petals from beautifully dyed thin silk by hand is a very delicate and elaborate task and the craftspeople who make them are now elderly. As the number of maiko has decreased so has the demand for kanzashis, and unfortunately it is now almost impossible for a family to make a living from their production. However, people recognize the beauty of kanzashis when the actually see them.

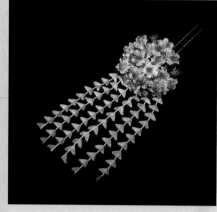

January: The decoration for the January kanzashi varies every year, although it always represents something related to the New Year. It was a *koma* (spinning top) in 1999. Top-spinning originally came from China and became popular among noblemen in the Heian Period. Later, in the Edo Period, it was played widely. Today it is still a children's New Year game, but its popularity is in decline. For the New Year celebrations, the maiko puts on a kanzashi made with dried ears of rice, with a small paper decoration of a white eyeless pigeon on her right. The maiko paints in one of the eyes and asks someone whom she likes to paint the other eye.

February: All over the country in February there are gatherings for viewing the plum blossom, which symbolizes the approach of spring. Daffodils are also worn in this month and in March.

March: The decoration of the kanzashi in March is a combination of rape blossoms and butterflies. Rape blossoms do not bloom until April, although it depends on the region, but adapting it early anticipates spring.

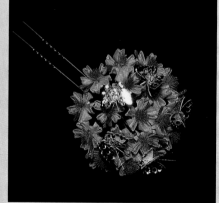

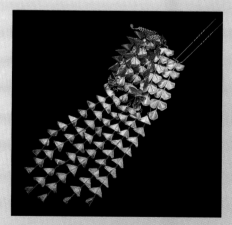

April: There are two kanzashis for the month, cherry blossoms and silver butterflies. In Japan, early April is the season for cherry-blossom viewing. The silver butterflies anticipate early summer.

May: Purple-coloured wisteria and different coloured irises are May's kanzashi motifs.

June: There are two kinds of decoration for this month. One is a combination of willow and a wild pink flower, the other is the hydrangea. June in Japan is the rainy season. Rain and pastel-coloured hydrangeas as well as fresh green willow symbolize the month.

July: An *uchiwa* is a round Japanese fan and one of the necessities for summer, in and out of the home. The uchiwa is used for this month's kanzashi but, in addition, the maiko uses a special kanzashi during the Gion festival. These change every year, one example consisted of a dragonfly and swirl of water.

August: Eulalia (Japanese pampas grass), or morning glory represent August. The kanzashi with silver-coloured eulalia is for the senior maiko, one with pinkish silver eulalia is for the younger maiko. August's other kanzashis incorporate morning glory, the flower that symbolizes summer in Japan.

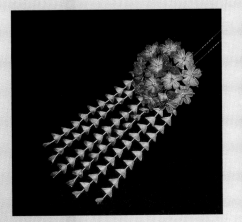 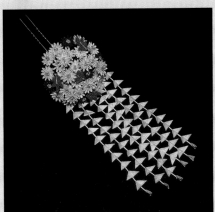 

September: September's flower is the Chinese bell-flower. It is a dark violet colour and represents the season when autumn's coolness begins to be felt.

October: Chrysanthemums are October's symbol. The flowers are loved by the Japanese and there are many exhibitions of them and even dolls made from them.

November: Scarlet maple leaves are the symbol of the month, representing the transition from late autumn to winter. Viewing the autumn leaves is as popular in Japan as cherry blossom viewing in April and Kyoto, in particular, is full of tourists at this time.

December: Rice cakes (*mochi*) are usually made in December and kept for the New Year holidays. There is a practice of decorating a tree with rice cakes (which are supposed to look like white flowers) called *mochibana*. This practice is echoed in the artificial mochibana attached to the kanzashi. The December kanzashi also has two small tags called *maneki*. Maiko visit the special kabuki performances at the Minamiza Theatre and each asks two actors she likes to sign their names on these tags. These symbolize the sign-boards called maneki in front of the theatre, on which the names of the kabuki actors are displayed

The geiko wears a kanzashi with two pointed pins and decorations attached. Such hair decorations were originally a form of self-protection – the geiko could strike at someone with the pin if she was in danger. For the summer season (June to September) the geiko's kanzashi is made from jade worn with a white or silver comb; for autumn, winter and spring (October to May) it is made from coral stone and worn with a tortoiseshell comb.

The geiko's hairstyle is not as colourful and bright as the maiko's, but in its understated way it is intended to represent the refined charm of the mature woman.

A maiko applying her eye makeup.

Make-up

When they attend the banquets, maiko and young geiko who have been in service less than three years after their erikae, always wear the long trailed kimono with katsura, white make-up and geta. If any element of this four-piece set is lacking, they would be a laughing stock throughout the hanamachi.

After three years' service, the geiko attends the ozashiki in the ordinary ankle-length kimono, with simple make-up and without a katsura, in which case she looks like any other woman similarly attired. The geiko who is over thirty only wears a long trailed kimono with white

The cosmetics used by the maiko and geiko.

make-up, geta and katsura when she performs a dance requiring such attire. Customers cannot ask her to wear this outfit unless they ask her to dance.

In order to apply white make-up, a maiko or geiko first smoothes bintsuke-abura on her face and the nape of her neck, from her hairline to her back. Bintsuke-abura for the face has different qualities to that used in the hair, it is an oil paste that is melted in the hand. Next, the white paste is mixed with water and applied with a brush, from the neck to the breast and from the nape to the back, using mirrors that are set against each other in order to see the back view. On the nape, two lines are usually left unpainted and on special occasions, such as ceremonies, three lines. After the painting is finished, powder is rubbed gently on the skin with a puff. Then the eyebrows are pencilled in. Maiko and geiko do all this very skilfully. If they do not draw the eyebrows properly, they have to remove all their make-up and start again, as, unlike normal foundation, it is not possible to make a partial adjustment to this make up.

On the day of a maiko's debut, her onesan or a professional make-up artist will apply the girl's make-up, but from the following day she has to do it herself. Early in her career, the maiko draws the eyebrows and the lines around her eyes in red, (although there may be some variation according to the hanamachi). As time progresses she mixes black with the red, gradually adding more black than red. Eventually, as a geiko, she will draw her eyebrows and eye-lines only in black.

The lip colour the maiko and geiko use comes in a small stick that is melted in water after which crystallized sugar is then added to give the cosmetic lustre. Originally, the rouge was stored in a pretty painted clamshell of the kind that is now sold as a souvenir in Kyoto. In Gion-Kobu, for the first year after her debut, a maiko paints only a little lip colour on the lower lip. This may be based on the belief in the past that small lips called *ochobo-guchi* were more attractive. At first, the geiko also paints her lips smaller than they really are although, after a while, as her make-up becomes clear and distinct, she paints her lips fully.

Artistic Accomplishments

Maiko and geiko have to continue to learn, and practice, music, dance and other artistic accomplishments throughout their career, irrespective of their age. This is indicated clearly in their names: maiko – woman of dance – and geiko – woman of art. Top class teachers usually come to the hanamachis to teach the maiko and geiko. There have also been schools for maiko and geiko in the hanamachis since the nineteenth century.

A geiko learns to play the *taiko* drum.

Artistic Accomplishments

n the hanamachi schools maiko and geiko take lessons in various artistic disciplines: musical instruments, such as *ookawa* (big hand drum), *kotsuzumi* (small hand drum), *taiko* (drum), *fue* (Japanese flute) and *shamisen* (three-stringed instrument); traditional dancing; narrative and recitative songs and Noh theatre. Those subjects not included in the school

Even the correct way to open a door is an important part of a geiko's training. This geiko is entering a room at the Yasaka Nyokoba Gakuen School in Gion-Kobu.

Geiko learning *odori* (dance).

curriculum, such as haiku (a style of Japanese verse, in which the poems contain just seventeen syllables), are taught on an individual basis.

Today, there are three maiko and geiko schools in Kyoto. They are Yasaka Nyokoba School in Gion-Kobu, Kamogawa School in Ponto-cho and Higashiyama Women's School in Miyagawa-cho. Gion-Higashi used to have the Mima School, but it was closed because of the fall in the number of maiko and geiko there. In Kamishichiken and Gion-Higashi, visiting teachers give lessons in the Kamishichiken Dance Theatre and in the office building of the Gion-Higashi Geiko Association.

The origin of the schools in Gion-Kobu and Ponto-cho can be traced back to the establishment of the female workers' training schools in 1872, a measure taken by the Meiji Government following the abolition of the obligatory term of service (*nenki-boko*) often imposed on the maiko, geiko, geisha, and other female entertainers, as well as on prostitutes. The government's educational reform provided opportunities for such women, so that they felt they had something to offer should they marry or wish to work outside the hanamachis. In Kyoto, the Kyoto Prefectural Nyokoba school, was established in 1871 (later the Kyoto Prefectural High School for Girls) – the first female school in Japan.

Practice

School hours in the hanamachis, like in schools elsewhere in Japan, generally run from ten or eleven in the morning to three in the afternoon. Lessons and

Dance lessons for the geiko, with the traditional accessories – the fan and the parasol.

practice are on a selective basis, according to individual interests and needs. Unlike most ordinary schools where desks and chairs are arranged in rows, the hanamachi classrooms, which are few and large, have tatami mats on the floor.

When the maiko arrives at school, she first greets the elder geiko already engaged in practice. Even actions such as opening doors, addressing her elders, and entering and leaving a room, are considered part of a maiko's training. Lessons are given on a group basis and those who make slow progress or do not put in sufficient effort will be told to practice in their own time.

One woman living near an okiya told me that until the 1960s some maiko who did not make progress in their dancing or in other artistic accomplishments were forced by their elder geiko to practice in the garden, starting at 5am in summer and 6am in winter. Sometimes elder geiko struck them if they were not performing well. Such harsh training, which was meant to benefit the student, would not be acceptable to day. Nowadays the maiko would not put up with such treatment and would simply leave the profession.

There is a traditional belief in Japan that the best time to start artistic training is at the age of six, plus six months and six days. This is based on the notion that art is not acquired through theory, but through practice, and it is better to start early so that the art becomes part of the body. Fewer and fewer girls start their learning at an early age and there has been a big drop in those accomplished in traditional music. However, according to one elderly geiko who was brought up in a Kyoto hanamachi, there are still many famous teachers and the maiko and geiko are proud to be able to take lessons from them. Until forty or fifty years ago, young girls in the hanamachis used to go to their teachers' house to take lessons, she remembered. It was part of their life – and she still retained pleasant memory of that, as she did of seeing the kabuki plays at the Minamiza Theatre for free, when she was introduced by her teachers.

However, the social environment in which such artistic accomplishment flourished in Kyoto has changed, even in the hanamachis where the traditions still remain.

Musical Instruments

Although there are many kinds of artistic accomplishments that the maiko and the geiko may acquire, it is mainly music and dance that they practice and take lessons in at school. When a maiko becomes a geiko, she has to improve her accomplishments intensively – the appeal of the geiko is in her refined elegance and accomplishment in art and in her manners. As time passes, some geiko specialize in dance and are called *tachikata* in some hanamachis. Others, called *jikata*, concentrate on playing instruments or on reciting Japanese ballads.

Taiko: One of the main musical instruments for traditional Japanese folk music, the taiko was originally called *tsuzumi* (hand drum). The name changed after ancient court music called *gagaku* came to Japan from China. The taiko consists of *do* (body), *kawa* (leather surface) and *shirabe* (flax strings). Its sound is adjusted by tightening the strings. The taiko is played on a stand,

TOP TO BOTTOM: **kotsuzumi, kane and shamisen.**

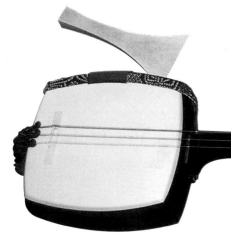

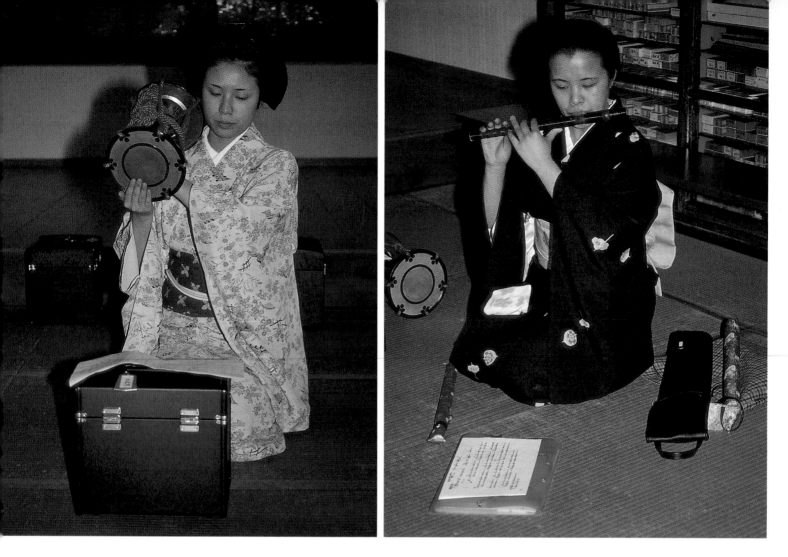

Left: **A maiko learning the kotsuzumi.**
Right: **A geiko learning the fue.**

the leather surface struck with two sticks. The kind of taiko used in the hanamachis is called *shimedaiko* (screwed up drum) and is made of zelkova wood and cow leather.

Kotsuzumi: The surface of the *kotsuzumi* (small hand drum) is made from horse leather, although in rare cases it may be deer hide. Leather made from a young horse that has not been strenuously exercised is considered to be the best quality. The body of the kotsuzumi, which is made of cherry wood, is fastened with flax strings both vertically and horizontally. The kotsuzumi is played on the right shoulder, held in place with the fingers of the left hand and struck on the leather surface with the flat fingers of the right.

The **Ookawa** (big hand drum) is also called *ootsuzumi* and is used in both Noh theatre and traditional ballads. Horse hide is fixed on iron ring-frames on both sides by a thick flax cord. The body of the instrument is made of cherry wood, the inside hollowed to produce acoustic effects. The body is painted with black lacquer, but in some cases with elaborately designed gold and silver lacquers. The player sits on the floor or on a stool, holding the instrument on the lap with the left hand. The drum is struck with the fingers of the right, which have paper or deerskin tips. The player accompanies the drumming with a rhythmic accented call. In contrast to the kotsuzumi, the style of playing looks

powerful and masculine. As the ookawa is hit very hard, its leather can only be used for a few performances.

Elder geiko learn the shamisen.

Fue: Made of bamboo, the *fue* is a type of flute that can be of various lengths and have different numbers of holes. The fue usually used in the hanamachis has seven. There is always a steady stream of maiko learning this instrument and more than ten kinds are in use among maiko and geiko.

Originally from China, the **Shamisen** literally means "strings of three tastes". It has three strings and it is also called *sangen*. Various improvements were made during its development, and since the beginning of the Edo Period (1603–1867), the shamisen has been used in the music of art and in popular folk music.

The neck of the shamisen is made of Chinese quince wood or rosewood. There are three kinds of shamisens according to the thickness of the neck: thick (*futozao*), medium (*chuzao*) and thin (*hosozao*), each of which has a different sound. Players choose the one best suited to their music. The front surface is made of cat skin and the back of dog skin, although sometimes both surfaces are made of the latter. The strings are of silk and the plectrum (*bachi*) is of ivory, tortoiseshell or oak. Recently, ceramic plectrums have also been used.

The shamisen is often played for a lengthy period and has to be tuned regularly. To play the shamisen, a player holds the neck with the left hand, the

SHAMISEN MUSIC

There are many different ways to play shamisen music. It can be combined with a narrative song, (*sugatari*), played in an ensemble with other instruments, or it can accompany a dance performance. The shamisen player either narrates or recites while playing the shamisen, or accompanies a narrator or reciter.

In the hanamachis, shamisen music is usually played as an accompaniment to dance performances. The most popular forms of shamisen music performed by the geiko are: *tokiwazu* and *kiyomoto* (narrative pieces) and *nagauta*, *kouta* and *hauta* (recital pieces).

Nagauta is shamisen music that follows a long recitation of a story. Such music dates back to the seventeenth century. Among the popular pieces that represent this style are *"Fujimusume"* ("Young Woman Carrying Wisteria"), a colourful kabuki dance showing various postures of a young woman; *"Matsuno Midori"* ("Greenness of a Pine Tree"), a dance of a tayu and a kamuro; and *"Akino-irokusa"* ("Colourful Autumn"), a dance base around a seasonal flower.

Hauta is a short piece of music that first appeared in the seventeenth century. In the Kyoho Era (1716–36), it came to be played at banquets and in *ningyo-shibai* (puppet plays). The popularity of this style was at its height towards the end of the Edo Period. Popular pieces include *"Harusame"* ("Spring Rain") and *"Umenimo Haru"* ("Spring for a Plum Tree").

Kouta is a comparatively new kind of shamisen music. It derived from hauta at the end of the Edo Period and became popular in the Meiji Period, particularly among businessmen and those who were versed in artistic accomplishments. Initially it was an artistic entertainment at the banquet, but in the Taisho Period it came to be included in various programmes, including theatrical performances. Kouta containing a monologues also appeared. After World War Two, there was a kouta boom and performances were often organized in Tokyo and other big cities. There are now more than eighty grand masters of different kouta schools. Compared with other kinds of shamisen music, kouta has a quick tempo and a light rhythm with a witty recitation. As kouta pieces are usually short, they are often played at banquets by geiko. *"Gion-kouta"* is the most popular piece. Others such as *"Yozakura"* ("Cherry Blossom Viewing at Night") and *"Sinobu Koi"* ("Secret Love") are also well known.

Jiuta developed in the same period as nagauta. One of its characteristics is that it incorporates folk and popular songs of the Edo Period. There are many kinds of jiuta, the most representative being *"Kurokami"* ("Black Hair") which is played on the occasion of erikaes in Gion-Kobu.

Tokiwazu is one of the schools of *joruri* (Japanese ballad drama), and is also called *tokiwazu-bushi*. From the middle of the eighteenth century it developed as kabuki music in Edo, together with nagauta. It sometimes combines shamisen music with a narration, but in the hanamachis the music accompanies a dance.

Kiyomoto is also called *kiyomoto-bushi*, and was first performed by Itsukidayu Tomimoto II in 1814. The Master Tomimoto incorporated folk and popular songs in his work and produced a new school of music that suited the tastes of the inhabitants of Edo.

Gidayu or *gidayu-bushi* was founded by Gidayu Takemoto in 1648 in Osaka, and its development was linked with the puppet play. Gidayu is now also played for the kabuki performances and there are many gidayu concerts as independent events. Compared with tokiwazu and kiyomoto, gidayu has more narrative features.

instrument on the lap, and strikes the strings with the right hand, either with the plectrum or sometimes just the fingers.

The shamisen is a very complicated instrument to master and, today, there are few first-class exponents among the geiko of Kyoto. Those who specialize in the instrument are in great demand. For some performances shamisen players from outside the hanamachis have to be invited to take part to make up the requisite numbers.

When the shamisen first came to Japan, it was used for folk and popular music. However, as it became popular, it was introduced into many kinds of music (see box opposite). Gradually the instrument was favoured for artistic performances, developing in two directions. One was a narrative style of music (*katarimono*), which includes *joruri, gidayu, tokiwazu* and *kiyomoto*; the other was a recitative style (*utaimono*), which includes such styles as *nagauta, kouta, hauta* and *jiuta*.

Other Accomplishments

The distinctive theatrical style of **noh** includes *utai* (noh songs) and the playing of the kotsuzumi, ookawa and fue. Noh and the comic interludes called Kyogen that accompany it developed from eighth-century Chinese theatre and a style of comical mimicry popular in ninth-century Japan. Noh developed absorbing the rhythm of the *shomyo* (Buddhist chanting) and the dances of the Shirabyoshi. In Gion-Kobu, *shimai* – a style of noh dance that is performed in plain clothes and without the masks that usually typify the genre – is practised. It is a part of noh drama that is usually performed only by a main actor or, in rare cases, together with a child actor and a supporting actor, and consists of unaccompanied singing.

Shodo is a calligraphic art that developed in Japan. The characters are written with writing brushes in black ink, creating not just a message, but also an artistic work in its own right. A scroll of calligraphy is often hung in the

OPPOSITE: Geiko learn the shamisen in 1956.

Ocha (tea) and *Okashi* (confectionery) served at the tea ceremony. The confectionery should reflect the season, this image was taken during the month of November and so the sweet resembles a maple leaf turing red.

tokonoma, expressing the beauty of the seasons, a thought concerned with Buddhism, Chinese poetry, or a Japanese saying. At the Miyako dance festival, calligraphic works by maiko and geiko are displayed.

Kado, more often called *ikebana,* is the Japanese art of flower arranging. Kado developed conspicuously in the Azuchi-Momoyama Period in the latter half of the sixteenth century when, as the castles and residences of the feudal lords became larger and more ornate, flower arrangements became sophisticated, spectacular and colourful.

It was in the same period that the tokonoma became a feature in Japanese room. Ikebana was placed in these alcoves, thus becoming a integral part of this architectural style. The practice of placing a flower arrangement in the tokonoma in each room in the ochaya also dates from this period.

Sado

It was during the Nara Period in the eighth century that tea was first imported to Japan from China. The practice of drinking tea was first referred to in writing

Top: At a tea ceremony, a maiko presents a cup of tea and bows to her guest. Above: Ikebana.

The tea ceremony.

from the early Heian Period. The practice gradually became popular among the court nobles. In the Azuchi-Momoyama Period, Senno Rikyu (1522–91), a merchant in Sakai, near Osaka, established the tea ceremony as an artistic accomplishment. Shogun Hideyoshi Toyotomi often organized tea parties such as a grand tea party (*ocha-kai*) in Kitano, in Kyoto, and as a result many feudal lords learnt and practised the tea ceremony – *sado*.

The objective is not necessarily to enjoy drinking tea, but to display manners and etiquette, through which the individual's culture and personality are enhanced. Greeting, making tea, handling the tea bowl and utensils, appreciating the ikebana and kado, and enjoying the fragrance of the incense are all actions that are enacted in a ceremonial manner.

In the hanamachis in Kyoto, the tea ceremony is always arranged for such occasions as the Miyako and Kamogawa dance festivals in Gion-Kobu and Ponto-cho, where the maiko prepare and serve tea. Among the many tea ceremony schools Omote-senke and Ura-senke, both of which are offshoots of Senno-Rikyu, are well known but in the hanamachis, but most people learn the Ura-senke style.

Banquets and Performances

Ozashiki are the banquets at which the maiko and geiko entertain their customers. The word is also used to refer to the banqueting rooms in teahouses, which are floored with tatami, a practice introduced in the Muromachi Period (1336–1573) and based on the traditional *shoin-zukuri* architectural style. The characteristics of shoin-zukuri architecture, which was particularly popular in the Edo Period (1603–1867), are the tokonoma and *kazari-dana* (display shelf) in the main rooms, and the *fusuma* and *shoji* – the distinctive wooden-framed sliding doors covered with *washi* (traditional Japanese paper) – that partition the rooms. In such an ozashiki the customers can enjoy the artistic accomplishments of the maiko and geiko in a unique and historical atmosphere.

Dancers from Gion-higashi in performance.

Banquets and Performances

A man wishing to attend an ozashiki has to make a reservation in advance with the okasan of the ochaya. It is her duty to make all the necessary arrangements for the ozashiki. First she informs the okasan of the okiya of the reservation, who in turn informs the maiko and geiko. A direct request for an engagement to a maiko or geiko is not allowed, even after a geiko has become independent it is always routed through her okiya.

The conventions of ozashikis differ but usually the maiko and geiko dance, recite and play the shamisen for an invited group of men who also enjoy food, drink and skilled conversation from the women. A banquet begins at about six

o'clock in the evening and lasts for between one-and-a-half and two hours. (Although in some cases the maiko and geiko may stay longer without an extra charge.) The hanadai (charges) for the ozashiki, covering meals and drinks and all the expenses for the maiko and geiko, vary substantially, depending on the number of guests, the number of women who have entertained the men and the type of meals ordered. For a customer to be entertained alone with a full-course dinner from a top-class restaurant, the cost is enormously expensive. It is more common for men to attend the banquets in groups, sharing the cost of the evening among themselves. Some teahouses have a lounge with a bar, where guests are served with drinks and snacks, which is certainly less expensive. A geiko does not know beforehand what kind of guests a customer will bring to a banquet. If the guests are VIPs, they are often invited to a first-class *ryotei* restaurant to be entertained.

According to one man well acquainted with hanamachi culture, the ochaya's charges, very roughly speaking, are half those at high-class nightclubs

The Cherry Dance being performed in Gion-Kobu Kaburenjo (theatre).

with hostesses (which appeared during the days of the "bubble" economy) and twice as much of those at a snack bar which has one or two hostesses. It is very difficult to indicate costs for a banquet in general terms because it depends on various factors, for example: duration, the number of geiko and maiko attending and the style of kimono a geiko wears. In some cases the teahouse may ask for more money if a customer seems affluent.

The teahouse pays all the charges for the banquet on behalf of the guests, including the hanadai for the maiko and the geiko. Traditionally it was common practice in Kyoto for a customer to meet his debts twice a year, in July and December. Now, he – or the company if it has hosted a banquet – receives an invoice for what he owes and he transfers the money into the ochaya's account.

Entering an Ochaya

To make a reservation at an ochaya, a man has to have been formally introduced to it or already acquainted with it. Many Japanese men who might be interested in the world of the hanamachis have not been to an ochaya simply because they have no means of contact. If a man is introduced to a teahouse, the person who has introduced him assumes the role of guarantor – if the new guest was not to pay his bill, or behaved inappropriately, it would be his friend whose reputation was damaged and he would be held responsible.

In the hanamachis, everything is based on personal relationships and trust within an inner circle. A customer will not, therefore, introduce an acquaintance in whom he does not have complete confidence. Thus, the customers who come to the ochaya have gone through a kind of vetting process. It is believed in Gion that a person or a company with a good reputation in the ochaya would be reliable and trustworthy in business. Recently, the hanamachis have

started to become a little more accessible. A businessman staying at a hotel in Kyoto may be able to get a reservation at an ochaya if he is known to be successful and respectable. In an attempt to increase the number of customers to the hanamachis, the Kyoto Traditional Artistic Accomplishment Promotion Foundation was established, and in 1998 the Association of Friends for the Foundation. The aim or these organizations is to increase offer introductions to the ochayas in the five hanamachis with the objective that people will gain an appreciation of the traditional cultural aspects of a banquet involving geiko and maiko.

Nevertheless, there are fears about such change within the hanamachis. The teahouses value the relationship with their regulars highly and in order to render a good service, they restrict the numbers who are allowed access to them. If access to the hanamachis becomes easier, the fear is that long-standing customers might feel they no longer get special consideration – and the banquets would lose their exclusivity. There is another, more fundamental reason why some of the ochayas are cautious – the okasan of an ochaya considers those who attend banquets as guests in her home and so there is an understandable reluctance to entertain customers she does not know well.

But despite such resistance the hanamachis appear to be opening their doors to the outside world, albeit slowly.

Enjoying a Banquet

When a customer passes through the crested curtains of the ochaya, he finds himself in the serenity of the flagged entrance hall where running water trickles quietly. Here he takes off his shoes and walks down a polished wooden corridor to the banquet room. From the corridor he is able to view a well-

maintained small garden with stone lanterns and attractively arranged natural rocks and trees. Within the ochayas, most of which are two-storeyed, there are usually several ozashikis linked by corridors. Every ozashiki has a tokonoma, decorated to reflect the season.

Once all the guests are gathered, the maiko and geiko arrive. They sit in a formal manner at the entrance of the room, greeting the guests before entering. Usually there is a seating plan; elder and senior figures take the upper seats closest to the tokonoma, while the juniors take the lower seats nearer the entrance. The okasan comes to welcome the guests and the host. Then drinks are brought in, a toast is proposed and the banquet begins.

Maiko and geiko serve drinks to the guests and accept those offered to them, but they never eat anything at a banquet. Sake is exchanged among the guests, a tradition that is believed to promote mutual understanding and communication. Sake is also called *omiki* (meaning the god's sake) and is

Backstage at the Kamogawa Odori in Ponto-cho Kaburenjo.

often dedicated at shrines all around Japan. Until the 1950s, there were many small sake breweries in and around the hanamachis, but today most of them have disappeared. The sake of Fushimi, in the southern part of Kyoto, is especially well known in Japan, but the number of breweries there has also declined. Sake production is now in the hands of a few big breweries. Sake is still popular at banquets, as is beer, whisky, *shochu* (a spirit), wine and champagne.

After the toast, meals are served. During dinner the maiko and geiko dance, accompanied by shamisen music and recitals. Artistic performances at the ozashiki are not lengthy or over complicated, each song or dance will last for a few minutes, and is chosen from among nagauta, hauta or kouta (see pp. 86), often at the customer's request.

To attend and enjoy an evening in the ozashiki, it is advisable for a guest to have some understanding of the traditional artistic accomplishments of the

The Kitano Odori in Kamishichiken Kaburenjo.

hanamachi world, even if he is unable to perform them himself. Before World War Two many top businessmen learnt traditional Japanese music as a hobby and was able to recite the traditional ballads while the maiko danced or the geiko played the shamisen. Today, however, the lives of such businessmen, and the way they use their leisure time, have changed. Most are too busy to learn artistic accomplishments, many of the older geiko find it sad that today there are so few customers who can talk about and take a knowledgeable interest in their artistic performances. Historically, the artistic skills and interest of the customers were an incentive for the maiko and geiko, encouraging them to improve their own talents. Nowadays, those most interested in learning the traditional instruments or dances are elderly women.

Games are also enjoyed at a banquet. "*Ken*", which are games played with hands, are among the most popular. There are many variations, among them "*Yakyu ken*" – a baseball-style game; "*Meoto ken*" – a game for couples, and "*janken*" –the well-known children's game of stone, paper, scissors. Although many of the Ken games, which originated in seventeenth-century China, have disappeared, "Yakyu ken" is still popular and is played by customers and maiko or geiko to the rhythm of music. If the customer loses, he removes an item of clothing. If the maiko or the geiko loses, she drinks a cup of sake in one breath. Another musical game called "*konpira-fune-fune*" is popular. This starts with a slow tempo that becomes quicker and quicker. Whoever cannot keep up with the shamisen loses, and has to pay a penalty.

The rest of the time at the ozashiki is spent in conversation. It is stimulating and lively as a geiko meets many people from different walks of life and so has a wide stock of information and knowledge, as well as her own opinions. A geiko converses with the guests on equal terms, whatever their position.

Main Performances

Each of the five hanamachis has its own dance school: Inoue School in Gion-Kobu, Onoue School in Ponto-cho, Hanayagi School in Kamishichiken, Wakayagi School in Miyagawa-cho and Fujima School in Gion-Higashi. All, with the exception of Inoue, are nationwide schools. Each hanamachi has its own dance theatre, and in the cases of Gion-Kobu, Ponto-cho and Miyagawa-cho, schools for maiko and geiko, which are established as an annexe to these theatres.

Performances by the maiko and geiko are mainly held in spring and autumn. Starting with the *Miyako Odori* – the Cherry Dance – in the Gion-Kobu dance theatre, some of the performances that follow include the *Kamogawa Odori* (Kamo River dance) in Ponto-cho; *Kyo Odori* (Kyoto dance) in Miyagawa-cho; and *Kitano Odori* (North Field dance) in Kamishichiken.

Dance performances in the hanamachis are popular, not only with the people of Kyoto, but with tourists from all over Japan. Unlike dance performances in the teahouses these are spectacular presentations with many maiko and geiko participating. Kimonos and accessories are ordered specifically for these occasions, and are so colourful and unique that they can even be appreciated by those who know nothing about Japanese dance.

Maiko and geiko work very hard to prepare themselves for the performances – the dances are performed in teams of approximately ten, so everybody's movements have to be synchronized perfectly. During the dance seasons – which last for about a month in the case of the Miyako Odori – there are four performances a day, in addition to which the maiko and geiko have to attend banquets in the evening. There is no time for the women to relax, but all who participate in the dances find them a rewarding experience, helping them to improve their artistic ability.

Before each of the performances, a tea ceremony conducted. Maiko or geiko prepare and serve tea accompanied by the Japanese confection called *Omanju*. The small original ceramic saucer that is used in the ceremony can be taken home and some customers collect them.

The Cherry Dance

The best-known dance performance in the hanamachis is Gion-Kobu's Miyako Odori. Known outside Japan as the Cherry Dance, its history dates back to 1871, when the first Expo was held in Kyoto. This Expo was staged with the intention of revitalizing Kyoto, which had lost power and influence after Tokyo became Japan's capital. The following year, public artistic performances were presented as a follow-up to the Expo and Haruko Katayama, the third grand master of the Inoue School of Dance, composed the Cherry Dance at the request of Sugiura, the owner of Ichiriki, the most famous teahouse in Gion.

The first performance of the Cherry Dance was much more successful than expected – and as a result it became established as a popular annual event. Sugiura asked Haruko what kind reward she would like. In reply, she asked that the Inoue School be designated the sole and exclusive dance school in Gion –

today it remains the only dance school in Gion-Kobu, the most well-known of
Kyoto's hanamachis. Only a woman can inherit the Inoue School and likewise
its dances can only be learnt by women. But the influence of Noh on the
school's method of teaching means that its style has inherited brisk and
masculine movements.

Yachiyo Inoue IV is the current grand master of the school and was a pupil
there. She was born in Gion, started dancing at the age of four, and was
married at the age of twenty-five to Hiromichi Katayama, one of the
grandchildren of Haruko Katayama. In 1948 she mounted the first public
performance of the Inoue School at the Shinbashi Enbujo Theatre in Tokyo,
which ensured the school's fame throughout Japan. She is still very active,
together with her grandchild, Michiko Inoue.

The Miyako Odori takes place throughout April in the Gion-Kobu dance
theatre and for the inhabitants of Kyoto it heralds the coming of spring. The
dances of the maiko and geiko, dressed in colourful kimonos that are often
blue and green, form a spectacular scene, resplendent with flowers. Every year
new dresses are ordered as they are used more than a hundred times during
the Cherry Dance season and so are worn out at the end of it.

Performances are composed of eight scenes – the theme of which is
always the four seasons – each lasting five to ten minutes. The first act always
contains scenery that includes a silver-coloured fusuma in the nobleman's

A geiko dancing "Fuji-musume" at a performance for a dance teacher in Ponto-cho.

residence. Other scenery used includes elements such as snow, plum flowers, cherry blossoms, shrines and temples.

The repertoire may include extracts from the kabuki plays and such classic pieces as *Ushiwakamaru* (the story of Yoshitsune Minamoto, younger brother of Shogun Yoritomo Minamoto) and *Kaguyahime* (the story of a young girl from the moon). Some pieces are based on the narratives of *bunraku* (puppet shows). Thus, the dances are influence by many different genres of Japanese theatre and dance, a feature that is characteristic of the Inoue School.

On the left side of the stage, which is referred to as the west, a musical band called *ohayashi*, consisting of taiko, ookawa and kotsuzumi, is seated, while shamisen players are seated on the opposite (east) side. When the phrase *"miyako odori wa"* is sung by the players on the east, dancers appear from both sides, shouting *"yoiyasa"* (we are ready) and the Miyako Odori begins.

The staging of the Cherry Dance is complex because the impassioned passages of music and dance have to be executed in a very condensed style. The performances are, therefore, usually very dynamic and of a quick tempo.

Other Dances

Kamogawa-odori: This dance is held in Ponto-cho, on the left bank of the Kamo River every May. The dance was first performed in 1872, the same year as the first performance of the Cherry Dance. Ponto-cho adopted the Onoue

School to teach its dances. This school bases its teaching on kabuki, which, to the expert eye at least, is quite different to the Inoue style.

Kitano-odori: Kamishichiken's Hanayagi School was established in 1849 by Jusuke Hanayagi. Jusuke Hanayagi II tried to develop the school in a new way, organizing the students and posting the instructors all over Japan. As a result, about a quarter of those who learnt the Japanese dance belonged to the Hanayagi School, the characteristics of which are delicacy, brilliance and abundant variations.

Kamishichiken has always been close to the textile industry in the Nishijin area and is often pointed out by local customers that the dresses in Kamishichiken are more refined than anywhere else. Kimono makers and textile dealers in Nishijin think that the Kitano-odori, held in April, reaches the highest artistic standard in Kyoto and, among its sixteen geiko, some of the best dancers and players. The characteristics of Kitano-odori are theatrical staging and artistic tastefulness, rather than splendour.

Kyo-odori: The Miyagawa-cho dance is taught by the Wakayagi School, founded by Judo Wakayagi in 1893, when he became independent from the Hanayagi School. Kyo-odori takes place in April, and *Miyagawa-ondo* (Miyagawa-cho folk songs), a favourite among local people, are played there.

Gion-odori: The Fujima School in Gion-Higashi is the second-largest dance school and has a long history and tradition. The founder was Kanbei Fujima, a composer of theatrical performances during the eighteenth century. Many dances related to the kabuki style of theatre are performed at the Gion-odori in November. These stagings, including the Miyako Odori, are composed of eight scenes. The Gion-Higashi-kouta is performed as the finale by all the maiko and geiko.

In addition to the above-mentioned main public performances in the five hanamachis, there are many other performances of various kinds including the *Yukata-kai* in Ponto-cho in August which involves the maiko or geiko performing in their summer kimonos to instrumental music.

In June, a joint two-day public performance of the five hanamachis is held in the Kyoto Kaikan Hall. The programme consists of six parts: the first five those of the individual hanamachis, the sixth a joint performance by maiko from all of them. Afterwards, a banquet, which the general public can attend is organized at Japanese restaurants in each hanamachi. The joint performance and banquet are sponsored by the Kyoto Hanamachi Association, the Ookini Foundation and Kyoto City Tourism Association.

In autumn, there are also performances. These are less spectacular than the spring public performances with fewer participants and smaller-scale stages. However, some believe them to be more attractive and worth seeing for those who are interested in artistic accomplishments.

Gion-Kobu's autumn dance, Onshu-kai.

The variety of performances in Kyoto's hanamachis is something that is very unique to the city. In April, May, October and November, the hanamachis put on several performances for tourists and other spectators in which the maiko and geiko participate. It was after October 1964, when the bullet train services were opened between Tokyo and Osaka, that tourists began to come to the performances in Kyoto. Access to Kyoto from other big Japanese cities became possible in little more than two hours, where previously it had taken up to eight.

The atmosphere of the public performances, such as Miyako Odori and Kamogawa Odori, has changed with an increase in the number of tourists. In the past most of the spectators were familiar with one another and came only from Kyoto – the few who came from Tokyo and elsewhere were mostly limited to dance teachers, people connected with dance, and the dannas of the geiko.

Seats were not allocated, people came to the theatre earlier and struggled to get those nearest the stage. The atmosphere was very lively and enjoyable for all concerned. However, after the inauguration of the bullet train services, prices went up and tickets were sold allocated. Spectators from Kyoto have become quieter in the presence of so many strangers – whose numbers increased still further after the Osaka Expo of 1970. Many they miss the atmosphere that once existed. Change continues to happen, and the hanamachi way of life is not immune, even as it comes to be more widely known and appreciated.

Calendar of Events

The year in Kyoto begins and ends with festivals, a considerable proportion of which are dedicated to the temples and shrines. As Kyoto was not a target of bombing raids during World War Two, the ancient sites in the city remained unharmed. The history and tradition of both Buddhism and Shintoism, which have disappeared in many parts of Japan, still remain part of the daily life of Kyoto something of which the city's inhabitants are extremely proud.

Jidai Festival, October 22.

Calendar of Events

I t is said in Japan that women are more pious than men. This is particularly true of the women of the hanamachis, whose lives are devoted to artistic accomplishment. Their links with the temples and shrines, where they participate in tea ceremonies and performances, matter a great deal to them. Furthermore, maiko and geiko have a deep respect for their teachers and ritual greetings to them are an important element of the annual calendar.

New Year Celebration (January 1–3): New Year is the biggest festival in the Japanese calendar. In Japan, New Year has much the same significance as Christmas in Western countries. During this three-day period, families get together and people visit relatives and friends and pray at the temples and shrines. *Otoso* (special sweet sake, spiced with several kinds of herbs) and *osechi* cuisine (assorted dishes including vegetables, peas and fish with many regional variations) are prepared and served.

Many maiko and geiko visit their parents during this period and most customers stay at home with their families, therefore the hanamachis are quiet at New Year, with very few banquets.

Commencement ceremony (January 7): By January 7, the maiko and geiko have returned to their hanamachis, and commencement ceremonies are held. On this day, both maiko and geiko wear the formal crested kimono in black. The maiko wears the kanzashi for the month of January, the geiko the coral winter kanzashi. Both also wear ears of rice at the front of their hair, the maiko on the right, the geiko on the left. It is believed that anyone who has three grains of this rice in their purse, wrapped in paper, will have good fortune and wealth. Customers therefore ask the maiko and geiko to spare them three grains of rice during the New Year season, .

At the Nyokoba School in Gion-Kobu, the maiko and geiko meet to pledge themselves to improve their talents. Those who have achieved the best results in their studies and earnings during the previous year receive honours, as does the outstanding ochaya. Finally, their geiko's dance teacher, the grand master of the Inoue School, performs a skilled and difficult dance entitled *"Yamatobumi"*, which is based on a Japanese myth. It is performed with a fan in the left hand while a bell is rung with the right.

Hatsyuyori (January 13): On this day, in Gion-Kobu, maiko and geiko pay a visit to their grand master of dance, Yachiyo Inoue IV, for the New Year greeting and otoso and *ozoni* (rice cake soup) are served. During the visit, the women resolve to improve their dancing.

Setsubun and Obake (February 2–4): Setsubun is the day preceeding the first day of spring in the Japanese lunar calendar. People throw roasted soybeans, shouting "Fortune in, devils out". In doing so, they drive out evil spirits and invite good luck into their homes. This ceremony usually takes place at shrines and temples, but many families conduct it in their home. In the past, people also put grilled sardines and holly leaves at the front door in the belief that the smell would repel devils.

At the shrines in the hanamachis, maiko and geiko participate in this bean-throwing ceremony. It is believed that whoever has a bean thrown at them will have good fortune. Maiko and geiko also perform a dedicatory dance at Kyoto's shrines, particularly the Yasaka shrine.

For two days on and around Setsubun, an event called *obake* (disguise) takes place in the hanamachis. Once, on the day itself, young women prayed for a good match by changing their hairstyle. Disguises were also seen – for example, some elderly women wore the attire and make up that was meant for young girls. The practice no longer exists, but a similar event takes place in

A geiko prays at a Kamishichiken shrine.

the hanamachis. Maiko and geiko, in groups of two or three, go to banquets dressed as actors, television stars, heroes and heroines from popular movies or even Sumo wrestlers. When they enter an ozashiki, they are offered a cup of sake, which they are supposed to drink in one breath. Then they perform an original dance that is in keeping with their disguise. As they attend quite a few banquets during this period, they are likely to drink rather a lot. Customers may well also be in disguise. In some cases, customers dress in women's kimonos and entertain the maiko and geiko.

Ooishi-ki (March 20): This event is held at Ichiriki, the most well-known teahouse in Gion, which visited by Chief Retainer Kuranosuke Ooishi of the Akao Clan when he lived in seclusion in Yamashina, Kyoto. Ooishi is the hero of a famous Kabuki play called *Chushingura*, who on March 20 1703 committed suicide with forty-six colleagues, after having taken revenge for his clan lord. In his memory, the Ichiriki organizes a party, where the grand master Yachiyo Inoue IV performs a dance called *"Fukaki-kokoro"* ("Deep Heart"). Three geikos recite a ballad called *"Yado-no-sakae"* ("Prosperity of an Inn"), and at a tea ceremony for regular customers, the maiko and geiko serve hand-made *soba* (Japanese noodles).

Dedicatory Dance at the Heian shrine (April 16): The Heian shrine is dedicated to Emperor Kanmu (737–806), who transferred the capital from Nara to Kyoto in 794. In memory of this occasion, young maiko and geiko from Gion-Kobu perform three dances. This event coincides with the Cherry Dance festival so the women taking part in both events are extremely busy!

Miyabi-kai (early July): *Miyabi* means refined elegance, *kai* means gathering. The Miyabi-kai is a gathering where the maiko and geiko of Gion-Kobu pay a visit to the Yasaka shrine, at the beginning of the Gion festival. Together with their grand master, Yachiyo Inoue IV, they pray for progress in dancing skills. On this day, maiko and geiko all wear a new yukata made from cloth of the same patterns and colours, which are u sually coloured white and dark blue.

Gion Festival (July 1–31): The Gion festival is one of the three major festivals in Japan. It lasts a whole month, with many special events and programmes arranged. It originated during a plague in 869 when sixty-six long axes were erected as a prayer to expel the epidemic. As one of the events, the maiko dedicates the "sparrow dance" to the Yasaka shrine, which is based on an old folk tale about a sparrow whose tongue was cut after it ate rice paste made by an old woman. On July 17, a grand parade of thirty-two floats, nine of them mounted with a long decorative axe, proceeds through the main streets of the city, lasting for several hours. On July 24, Gion holds a dance parade, in which many women, including maiko and geiko wear hats adorned with flowers.

The Miyabi-kai of Gion-Kobu. The geiko go to the Yasaka shrine and pray for that they will be good at dance. This image dates from 1956.

Zuiki festival (October 4); the parade proceeds to the Kitano Tenmangu shrine in Kamishichiken. A maiko and geiko can be seen standing outside a teahouse.

Hassaku (August 1): Hassaku commemorates the day that the Shogun, Ieyasu Tokugawa (1542–1616) moved to Edo castle. The day was designated as the day of military commanders on which, thereafter, feudal lords had to come to the castle. On this day maiko and geiko visit their teachers and the teahouses. Kyoto is hot and humid in the summer, nevertheless, maiko and geiko wear formal black summer kimonos made from ro and decorated with five crests. Wearing such heavy formal wear in the heat indicates their resolve to improve their artistic talents.

Zuiki festival (October 4): A parade of sacred palanquins and floats decorated with various kinds of vegetables proceeds through the Kamishichiken streets on this day. This is a harvest festival for crops grown in the region, and is dedicated to the Kitano Tenmangu shrine nearby. The maiko and the geiko in the Kamishichiken hanamachi stand in front of the teahouses and welcome the parade.

Jidai festival (October 22): In 1895, the Heian shrine was constructed to commemorate the 1,100th anniversary of the transfer of the capital to Kyoto. Since then, a large-scale parade, composed of groups representing each historical period from the Heian to the Meiji, takes place in full traditional costumes.

The Kanikakuni Festival in Gion-Kobu. The maiko pray and offer chrysanthemums to the monument to Isamu Yoshii.

In 1950, a female group first took part in the parade. Since then the hanamachis of Gion and Ponto-cho have been responsible on alternate years for the female entry to the parade. The maiko and geiko dress up as beauties from each period, for example, as Onono Komachi, a female poet in the first part of the Heian Period who was referred to the "Paragon of Beauty"; as Shizuka Gozen, a former shirabyoshi and later mistress of Yoshitsune Minamoto, younger brother of Shogun Yoritomo Minamoto, in the Kamakura Period; or as Tomoe Gozen, mistress of Yoshinaka Minamoto (1154–88), cousin of Shogun Yoritomo Minamoto.

Kanikakuni Festival(November 8): This event commemorates Isamu Yoshii (1886–1960), a playwright and poet who loved Gion very dearly. Born the second son of a noble family in Tokyo, he spent almost all his assets in Gion. His literary works include "Gion anthology" and essays on the hanamachi including the maiko and geiko.

The word *Kanikakuni* is from the ancient Japanese meaning "one thing or another", but also "at any rate". The name of this event comes from Isamu Yoshii's well-known *waka* (a Japanese verse of thirty-one syllables), which begins with the word, *kanikakuni* and continues, "Gion is my heart, When in bed, water is running underneath the pillow". Isamu Yoshii used to stay at an

The stone in which Isamu Yoshii's waka verse is engraved.

ochaya called Daitomo, located across the Shirakawa River in Gion, which is where he composed this verse. The okasan was Taka Isoda, a literary geiko who was very popular among men of literature in her time. The area has long gone. During World War Two, many teahouses in this area were confiscated and knocked down to prevent the spread of fire and, although teahouses were reconstructed after the war, there is no longer a teahouse across the river.

Maiko and geiko eating Japanese soba noodles at the Kanikakuni festival.

In 1955 a stone monument on which his verse is carved was erected at the old site. On November 8 every year, the anniversary of this monument's unveiling, people gather there to commemorate the poet and watch the maiko and geiko of Gion-Kobu make an offering of chrysanthemums. Then, at a tea ceremony in front of the monument, they serve hand-made soba noodles. A hanging scroll on which Isamu Yoshii's verse is written, together with photographs of him, are also displayed.

Okencha (December 1): This tea ceremony is held at the Kitano Tenmangu shrine and in its vicinity on December 1, and is an event for which the grand masters of tea ceremony schools gather. Kamishichiken dance theatre is one of the venues and the maiko and the geiko prepare and serve tea.

Kaomise-soken (early December): The annual Kaomise kabuki performance is held for twenty-six days at the Minamiza Theatre, located at the site where Okuni, founder of the kabuki dance, presented her first performance in 1603. This performance introduces the cast for the next year. On the fourth and fifth days, the maiko and geiko, dressed in their colourful formal crested kimonos, sit in the boxes and view the performance. This group viewing is called *soken*.

Koto-hajime (December 13): Koto-hajime means the commencement of work. Although it is still December, the maiko and geiko visit their teachers and their minarai-jayas, to express their gratitude for year that has passed and their greetings for next. They usually take round "mirror" rice cakes called *kagami-mochi*, which are specially made for the New Year celebration. In Gion, Yachiyo Inoue gives a fan from the Inoue School to each maiko and geiko as they visit her house, to encourage them to do their best for the coming year.

Okotousan and okera flame (December 31): In the language of Kyoto, *okotousan* means "such a busy moment with so many things to do". It is the phrase the maiko and geiko use as they travel around the hanamachis offering greetings at the teahouses that engage them. The okasan gives each of them a special-shaped bag called *fukudama* (fortune ball) in which she puts small gifts such as a paper-made balloon and a small notepad. One of the sights that can be viewed in Kyoto on New Year's Eve is that of the maiko and geiko carrying many fukudama in their hands as they walk along the busy streets of the city.

During New Year's Eve and into the early morning hours of New Year's Day, many people go to the Yasaka shrine and bring back a straw torch lit from a sacred *okera* flame; this is a kind of plant which produce a special odour when it is burnt and was once believed to combat epidemics. Having brought home the burning torch, people use it to light the fire to cook *ozouni*, the New Year's special soup with rice cakes. It is believed that cooking with the okera flame will bring luck for the coming year. Some maiko and geiko who stay in Kyoto participate in this.

Modern Life in the Hanamachis

Gion, the major hanamachi in Kyoto, was at its peak in the first half of the nineteenth century, before it was divided into Gion-Kobu and Gion-Higashi. At that time, there were about 700 teahouses and more than 3,000 geiko in the area. Although the number of maiko and geiko has decreased, it still attracts the attention of people both inside and outside Japan. There is a move to promote an understanding of the splendour of the hanamachis in people from outside of them.

A geiko takes a moment to read about the outside world.

Modern life in the Hanamachis

From the late nineteenth century through to the middle of the twentieth century, Japan was invariably involved in conflict: the Japan–China War (1884–95), the Japan–Russia War (1904–05), World War One (1914–18), the Japan–China War (1937–45) and World War Two (1941–45). On the whole, the hanamachis of Kyoto prospered throughout, particularly in the period up to World War One when the Japanese economy boomed. The number of geiko in Gion at this time exceeded a thousand. In fact, their kimonos, kanzashis and footwear were often ordered by the military authorities. High-ranking army officers, businessmen in the shipping, aircraft and mining industries, and merchants in trade, all had the

ABOVE: Maiko help to publicize events at the Minamiza theatre.
OPPOSITE: A geiko out shopping.

balance of economic power and indulged in luxurious banquets in the hanamachis. In the barracks, which the maiko and geiko visited to entertain the soldiers, there was always abundant food, liquor and cigarettes. One elderly geiko recalls that she looked forward to such visits, where life was very different to that of ordinary citizens.

In 1923 a massive earthquake killed over a hundred thousand people in and around Tokyo and the surrounding area and destroyed over sixty per cent of the buildings in the city. The Japanese economy and the industrial sectors were struck a disastrous blow – and the hanamachis felt the impact. The economic situation had begun to recover when the Japan–China War broke out, swiftly followed by World War Two and, initially at least, the hanamachis were revitalized, thronged with high-ranking military and businessmen from the war-related industries. The geiko and maiko resumed their visits to the army barracks. The third grand master of the Inoue School of Dance, Haruko Katayama, led visits to the military hospitals to console the wounded. Kimono makers and merchants prospered and it was reported that Gion-Kobu donated two military planes to the air force.

**ABOVE LEFT AND OPPOSITE: Mobile phones are almost a part of the geiko "look" in modern times.
ABOVE: This geiko has created her own internet sight and regularly updates it with information about the hanamachis.**

The Miyako Odori festival continued to be held, with performances dedicated to the national glory. However, as the war situation deteriorated, business in the hanamachis fell away and was then discontinued completely. Maiko and geiko, who had equipped themselves with wartime trousers called *monpe* so they could help with fire-prevention activities in the event of air-raids, left the hanamachis, many returning to their home towns. In Gion, Katuzo Nakajima, then deputy representative of the Gion-Kobu Teahouse Association, was so concerned about their disappearance, he tried to get them jobs in the nearby munitions and other factories so they would stay. In Ponto-cho, the dance theatre was converted into a work centre for the production of military badges and some geiko worked there. One geiko recalls that she was very good at sewing and worked very hard for the army during this time.

Such organizations as the Gion Kokubo-Fujinkai (Women's Defence Association) and the Ponto-cho Seinen-Fujinkai (Young Men and Women's Association) were formed by the okasans and the geiko. They sent comfort packages to the front which, besides daily necessities and magazines, included good luck amulets and *senninbaris*, which are belts sewn by a thousand people as a prayer for good luck.

A considerable number of ochayas in the hanamachis were destroyed on the orders of the military – wooden buildings were a potentially serious fire risk if Kyoto were bombed. The streets in Gion along the Shirakawa River changed dramatically. In Ponto-cho, more than thirty teahouses were demolished and the area transformed into a park. Many other ochayas that were not pulled down were left empty as the inhabitants took refuge in the countryside. When the war ended in 1945, there were an estimated 350 geiko left in Gion. The hanamachis partly reopened the following year and, despite the suffering Japan experienced in the immediate postwar years, quickly became active once more. The clientele had changed, however, and the customers were now black marketeers and profiteers – and officers of the Occupation Forces. Sake was rationed and inferior in quality, but life in the hanamachis, one geiko remembers, was a "dream" compared with other peoples'.

The dance theatre in Gion-Kobu was requisitioned by the Occupation Forces and the Miyako Odori dance festival was interrupted for six years after 1943. It restarted at the Minamiza Theatre in 1950, with the best musicians and narrators of nagauta, joruri and tokiwazu participating. Men of literature such as Isamu Yoshii and Jun-ichiro Tanizaki wrote the music, which was performed by the most senior geiko.

When the Occupation Forces came to Ponto-cho, a maiko called Ichikoma was asked to appeal to them not to requisition the theatre. This she did, crying bitterly, and was so successful the officers left the theatre alone – but it was used as a dancehall for the Occupation Forces.

Postwar Days

Many of the stories about geisha, geiko and maiko published in other countries tend to suggest that they live in an unchanging time warp. But since World War Two, life has changed considerably. Among other things, maiko and geiko no longer come from poverty-stricken families, but choose their profession of their own volition and retire from it of their own free will. The miserable situation of the past, which forced young women to work in the hanamachis, no longer exists.

What has not changed is the heritage and strength of the hanamachis. The festivals and ceremonies of Shintoism, Buddhism and the Japanese lunar calendar that have declined or disappeared elsewhere, continue to be an important element of daily hanamachi life. The traditional artistic accomplishments continue to be learnt, the customs relating to kimono wearing observed, and respect for human relations and the hanamachi heirarchy, as well as discipline and manners, maintained. Today, when most people deal with others by telephone or e-mail, the maiko and geiko still pay personal visits, and the practice of offering written congratulations or thanks still goes on – thoughtful considerations that are rare outside the hanamachis, but still demanded inside them. Although elderly geiko and the okasans complain

that nowadays the maiko and the younger geiko tend to neglect good manners and etiquette, hanamachi society is still an area where decorum matters.

A young geiko pointed out to me that the hanamachi is not enclosed by walls and that she can go out any time, for example, to a movie or shopping. However, she said, whereas when she first came to her hanamachi and found it out of step with the world, now she finds the world out of step with the hanamachi. It intrigues maiko and geiko who still live in the okiyas how an independent geiko can become used to living in an apartment outside. Everyone in the hanamachi community takes pride in their difference.

Opening Up

While the hanamachis have been endeavouring to maintain their character, there is a move to extend an understanding of their traditions and splendours to as many people as possible. Kyoto has a history of more than twelve hundred years as the political capital of Japan as well as her cultural centre and there is an emerging interest in re-evaluating the maiko, the geiko – and the hanamachis – as living cultural traditions. This, however, is taking place against

Two of the most familiar symbols of Japan juxtaposed: the maiko and the bullet train.

a background of gradual decline. Regular customers are fewer, as are the men who can afford to be, or even want to be, dannas, and the younger generation feels more at home in karaoke bars. Maiko numbers are still falling. And it becomes ever more difficult to train talented maiko and geiko in artistic accomplishments – in which the interest of the Japanese as a whole has waned. This may be partly because more stress has been put on Western art and music in postwar education. Many schools have brass bands and drum-fife bands, but very few have traditional music clubs for such instruments as the kotsuzumi, ookawa and shamisen.

In such circumstances, the Foundation for the Promotion of Traditional Artistic Accomplishments was created in Kyoto in 1996 to foster interest. Popularly called *Ookini-Zaidan* (ookini is a polite expression of thanks in the language of Kyoto) the foundation has set up the Association of Friends, with a view to widening the support base. For an annual membership fee of thirty thousand yen, members receive invitations to the two hanamachi dance festivals, discount tickets for the joint performance of the five hanamachis, the offer of a special seat at the Jidai festival in October, and an invitation to the annual party. Members are also introduced by the foundation to an ochaya for a banquet. Further, on the occasion of the joint performance of the five hanamachis in June, each hanamachi organizes an ozashiki at a ryotei for

A maiko indulges in a popular soft drink.

which anyone can buy a ticket at a cost of twenty five thousand yen, through the Kyoto City Tourism Association. In 1996, the Ookini Foundation started the new initiative of awarding particularly talented geiko as "holders of traditional artistic talents" – with a view to encouraging all geiko and maiko to improve their art. This was reported in the *Asahi Shimbun*, a national newspaper, under the heading "Living Treasure in Kyoto". In that year, six geiko were given the honour, followed by six more in 1997.

Today geiko and maiko participate in goodwill missions to overseas countries with government or civil service officials. They pose for posters, calendars and postcards and participate in campaigns for many organizations and companies. The maiko – who are unique to Kyoto – in particular play an important role in tourism and cultural promotion programmes, such as the kimono shows and the Kyoto manufacturing exhibition. They often travel to various parts of Japan to attend exhibitions and fairs and they perform at restaurants and hotels when VIPs and missions visit Kyoto from overseas. Nowadays, their performances are often held in hotels on the occasions of large banquets or receptions where a stage is set up. On such occasions, full-scale performances by some fifteen maiko and geiko can be given, accompanied by the shamisen and other musical instruments – a challenging opportunity to show all their skills, something they cannot do in a small ozashiki.

Some geiko are active in other areas. For example, Tamaryo of Kamishichiken has a career as a fashion advisor and supervizes the manufacture of a kimono and obi under her own name. Other geiko have been to New York for fashion shows, or to south Asia and Europe to perform on stage. There is even one geiko who has launched a website on the Internet and posts information about the hanamachis. Some geiko are learning or have learnt English in the expectation that more customers will come from overseas.

It is interesting to note that there now are more than twenty studios and beauty saloons in Kyoto where customers can be dressed as maiko or geiko. The idea was introduced in various magazines several years ago and has become very popular with tourists who, when they are attired and made up, have their photos taken and walk – or take a rickshaw – around the streets of Kyoto. The age of female clients ranges from the teens to the seventies and some come to Kyoto expressly for this purpose. Today, many cosmetic stores and accessory shops in the hanamachis are crowded with female tourists, the majority of them young – indicating a growing curiosity in the world of the maiko and geiko. This curiosity may be based on nostalgia for a cultural heritage that no longer exists in day-to-day life but, certainly, the maiko and the geiko have become widely known in Japan. And they are becoming so in other countries.

The challenge for the hanamachis in the future is to capitalize on this growing interest, but without letting it undermine its culture and traditions. As they search for a new, positive image, the geiko and maiko seem to be at an important turning point. While their unique characteristics should be maintained as a precious cultural heritage, new directions must be explored for them to survive in twenty-first century.

The maiko and geiko are used to posing for tourist photographs.

Glossary

Note: At the time of going to press 170 yen = £1 sterling/100 yen = US$1

awase – a kimono with a lining.

danna – a patron, who supports a geiko or geisha, by giving financial assistance.

erikae – the ceremony at which the maiko becomes the geiko. The neck band – *eri* – changes from the red of the maiko to white.

geiko – Literally meaning "woman of art"; the Kyoto term for female entertainers, who train in the traditional Japanese arts. Commonly known as geisha elsewhere, although the standards of training in Kyoto are far more stringent than in other Japanese cities.

geta – wooden clogs.

goshugi – tips passed on to the maiko or geiko; they are always presented in an envelope.

hanadai – literally meaning "flower charges"; the charges made for a geiko or maiko's time; they make up the womens' salary.

hanamachi – the licensed areas of Japanese cities in which the geisha or geiko and (in Kyoto) maiko live and entertain. In Kyoto there are five hanamachis: Ponto-cho, Gion-Kobu, Gion-Higashi, Miyagawa-cho and Kamishichiken.

hiki-iwai – the celebration of retirement when a geiko or geisha leaves the hanamachi to either marry or take up another profession.

ichigen-san okotowari – strangers or chance customers who are not admitted into the teahouses.

ikebana – the art of traditional Japanese flower arrangement, also called *kado*.

iromuji – a kimono without patterns.

jikata – a geiko or geisha who specializes in music.

jimae geiko – a geiko who has left the okiya after completing her *nenki* (*see below*) and makes her livelihood independently.

kabuki – a traditional style of Japanese theatre in which men play all the roles; it shares much of its history with that of the hanamachis in Kyoto – both traditions originated in Gion.

kaburenjo – dance theatre; each of the five Kyoto hanamachis has its own.

kamon – the family crest that appears on formal kimonos. Every Japanese family has one and in within the hanamachis, each okiya and ochaya will also have its own "family" crest.

kanzashi – hair pins. Those worn by the maiko change with the occassion or season and are very flamboyant, those worn by the geiko are less colourful.

katsura – wig.

komon kimono – kimono with small patterns.

kuro-montsuki – the black, formal kimono with crests.

kyo-yuzen – a traditional method of dyeing fabric, which is traditionally washed in the Kamo river in Kyoto. The fabric is of the highest quality.

maiko – the apprentice geiko, literally "woman of dance"; maiko exist only in Kyoto and have no counterpart elsewhere in Japan.

minarai-san – apprentice maiko, who learns the ways of the hanamachi by living together with the maiko and geiko in an Okiya and going to school there.

Miyako Odori – the Cherry Dance, the most famous and popular of the dances performed by the maiko and geiko in Gion-Kobu.

mizuage – the occasion on which a geiko or geisha loses her virginity; the term is an anachronism now as sexual matters are the business of the geiko or geisha alone.

nagauta – a style of Japanese ballad learned and performed by geiko and geisha on the shamisen.

nakai – serving women in the ochayas.

nenki – a maiko/geiko's period of service in the okiya.

obi – the sash worn around the kimono.

obi-age – the narrow strip of fabric that is seen above the maiko's sash, it is usually inside a geiko's.

obi-dome – the clasp attached to the front of the obi, the maiko's is called *pocchiri*.

obi-jime – the thin braid that ties around the obi.

ochaya – teahouse where banquets are held and where the geiko and maiko entertain their customers.

odori – dance.

ofuku – hairstyle worn by the elder maiko.

okasan – "mother" of the okiya or ochaya – all members of the hanamachi refer to her as such.

okiya – lodging house for the maiko and geiko during her nenki.

okobo – the high-heeled wooden clogs worn by the maiko.

omisedashi – the ceremony where a minarai-san becomes a maiko.

onesan – "elder sister", a role a geiko takes to pass on her experience to maiko and younger geiko.

oniisan – "elder brother", customers in the teahouses are generally addressed as this, although some are addressed as *"otosan"* (father).

otokosu – the only male profession within the hanamachis, the "kimono dresser". Only five now remain in Kyoto.

ozashiki – this can refer to either a banquet in an ochaya, or the traditionally styled banqueting room in which these are held.

pocchiri – sash clasp worn by the maiko.

ro – a delicate, loose weave silk fabric used to make summer kimonos.

sado – the tea ceremony.

sakko – the hairstyle worn in the month before the maiko becomes a geiko.

san san kudo – literally meaning "three times three exchange"; the ceremony at which a new maiko is joined in sisterhood with her "onesan".

sha – coarser than ro (*see above*), a silk made to use summer kimonos.

shamisen – three-stringed musical instrument studied and played by the geiko and the geisha.

shikomi san – the first stage or apprenticeship in an okiya, before a girl becomes *minari-san* (*see above*). She performs domestic duties, while living in the okiya and attending school.

shironuri – white paste make-up worn by the maiko and younger geiko.

shodo – the traditional Japanese calligraphic art.

tabi – socks with the the big toe separated.

tachikata – a geiko or geisha who specializes in dance.

tan – a traditional Japanese measurement for kimono cloth, measuring 37 centimetres wide by 12 metres long.

tatami – traditional straw or rattan matting.

tayu – entertainers in the Shimabara district of Kyoto; they are similar to *oiran* in Tokyo.

tokonoma – alcove found in traditional Japanese rooms, it always contains a floral display (*ikebana, see above*) and a hanging scroll.

ware-shinobu – hairstyle worn by the maiko during her initial period of training.

yukata – informal cotton kimono.

zori – cloth- or leather-covered sandals.

Index

Page numbers in italics refer to illustrations.

Ageya 11
Akao Clan 108
Akino-irokusa 86
Amaterasu-Oomikami 38
Asahi Shimbun 123
Association of Friends 95, 122
Awase 62, 124
Aya-ori 62
Azuchi-Momoyama Period 88, 89

Bachi 85
Banquet *16*, 21, 23, *23*, 27, *27*, 41,
   47, 48, 49, 52, 70, 77, 86, 91,
   92, 93, 94, 95, 96, 98, 99, 102,
   106, 108, 118, 123
Bean-throwing ceremony 107
Beer 97
Binaki 70
Bintsuke-abura 71, 77
Bira-kan 73
Buddhism 68, 105, 120
Bullet train *121*

Champagne 97
Charges 40
Cherry Dance *see* Miyako Odori
Chignon 40
Chikamatsu, Monzaemon 49
Chirimen 62
Chonin bunka 49
Chu-Sei era 49
Chushingura 108
Chuzao 85
Coat 68
Comic interludes 87
Commencement ceremony 106
Crest 68

Daikan 66
Daitomo 112
Dance festivals 122
Dance schools 99
Dango 17
Danna 17, 27, 40, 47, 51, 52, 54,
   73, 122, 124
Dedicatory Dance at the Heian
   Shrine 108
Disguise 107
Do 83

Ebisu 41
Edo castle 110
Edo Period 12, 17, 49, 73, 74, 85,
   86, 91
Eri 69
Erikae 44, *44*, *51*, 66, *66*, 69, 73,
   77, 86, 124
Erikae-danna 47
Expo 99

Family crests 63
Fan 70, *70*, *82*
Flower charges 40
Food boxes 41
Foundation for the Promotion of
   Traditional Artistic
   Accomplishments 122
Fue 80, *84*, 85, 87
Fujima school 99, 102

Fujima, Kanbei 102
Fujimusume 86, *101*
Fukaki-kokoro 108
Fukudama 113
Fushimi 97
Fusuma 91, 100
Futozao 85

Gagaku 83
Geiko-Kumiai 47
Geisha 49, 81, 120
Genroku Era 12, 49, 63 63
Geta 66, 70, *70*, 77, 124
Ghoshugi 27
Gidayu 86, 87
Gidayu-bushi 86
Gi-jo 49
Gindashi-abura 73
Gi-oh 49
Gion 9, 13, *13*, 15, *15*, 120
   Festival 29, 73, 75, 108
   hanamachi 38, 40, *51*
   Kokubo-Funinkai 119
   shrine 12
Gion-Higashi 15, 102
   Geiko Association 81
   hanamachi 10, 11, 30, 81, *91*,
      99, 115
   kouta 102
   Shinchi 15
Gion-Kobu 15, 17
   dance theatre 99, 120
   hanamachi 10, 11, *66*, 73, 77,
      80, 81, 86, 87, 89, 99, 100,
      103, 106, 108, *108*, 111, *111*,
      112, 113, 115, 118
   Kaburenjo 93
   Teahouse Association 119
Gion-kouta 86
Gion-odori 102
Gion-Otsubu 15, 17
Gion-Shinchi 13
Gohan-tabe 40
Gokagai 11
Goshugi 39, 41, 124
Gozen, Shizuka 111
Gozen, Tomoe 111
Gyoku-dai 49

Habutae 62
Hachimonji 49
Hada-juban 62, *62*
Haiku 12, 80
Hairstyle *51*, 70, 76
Haizen 15
Hakimono 66, 70
Hanadai 27, 40, 52, 93, 94, 124
Hanamachi 6, 7, 9, *9*, 10, 13, 20,
   21, 22, 27, 29, 30, 32, 34, 35,
   38, 39, 40, 47, *47*, 48, 49, 51,
   52, 55, 70, 71,77, 79, 81, 83,
   86, 89, 106, 111, 116, 118, *118*,
   119, 120, 121, 124
   Association Secretariat 38
   crest 17
   Gion 38, 40, 41, *51*
   Gion-Higashi 10, 11, 30, 81, *91*,
      99, 115
   Gion-Kobu 10, 11, *66*, 73, 77,
      80, *81*, 86, 87, 89, 99, 100,
      103, 106, 108, *108*, 111, *111*,

112, 113, 115, 118
Kamishichiken 11, 15, 16, 17,
   18, *27*, 30, *54*, 81, 99, 110,
   110, 123
Miyagawa-cho 11, 16, 17, 38,
   81, 99
Ponto-cho 11, 15, *16*, 17, *18*,
   38, 39, 40, 81, 89, 99, 111
Shimabara *10*, *11*, 12, *12*
   school 80, *80*, 81
Hanamikoji 9
Hanayagi school 99, 102
Hangyoku 49
Harusame 86
Hassaku 66, 110
Hassaku festival 29
Hatsuyuyori 106
Hauta 86
Heian Period 44, 49, 68, 74, 89,
   108, 110, 111
Higashiyama 12, 15
Higashiyama Women's School 81
Hiki-iwai 55, *55*, 124
Hima-wo-morau 52
Hira-ori 62
Hogaku 6
Hokan 49
Horeki Era 49
Hosozao 85
Hyottoko 41

Ichigenkin 11
Ichigen-san 6
Ichigen-san okotowari 27, 124
Ichikoma 120
Ichiriki 99, 108
Ihara, Saikaku 15
Ikebana 6, 88, *88*, 89, 124
Inoue IV, Yachiyo 100, 106, 108
Inoue School 99, 100, 101, 106,
   113, 118
Inoue, Michiko 100
Inoue, Yachiyo 113
Ippon 40
Iromuji 68, 70, 124
Isamu Yoshii Monument 111, *111*,
   113
Isoda, Taka 112
Issun 68

Janken 98
Japan-China War 116, 118
Japan-Russia War 116
Jidai Festival *105*, 110, 122
Jikata 83, 124
Jimae 23, 47, 124
Jiuta 86, 87
Joruri 86, 87, 120

Kabuki 16, 17, 40, 41, 49, 63, 66,
   75, 83, 86, 102, 108, 113, 124
Kaburenjo, Kamishichiken *97*, *100*
Kaburenjo, Ponto-cho 97
Kado *see* Ikebana
Kagami-mochi 113
Kagotsurube Sato-no-Eizame 49
Kaguyahime 101
Kamakura Period 111
Kamishichiken 102, *107*
   dance theatre 81, 99, 113
   hanamachi 11, 15, 16, 17, *18*, *27*,
      30, *54*, 81, 99, 110, *110*, 123

Kaburenjo *97*, *100*
Kamo River *15*, 16, 17, 63, 101
Kamo River dance *see* Kamogawa
   Odori
Kamogawa dance festival 89
Kamogawa Odori *96*, 101, 103
Kamogawa School 81
Kamon 63, 124
Kamuro 49, 86
Kane *83*
Kanikakuni Festival 111, *111*, 112,
   112
Kanmu, Emperor 108
Kanoko 71, 73
Kanoko-dome 73
Kanzashi 40, 43, 44, 62, 66, 73,
   76, 106, 116, 124
Kanzashi variations 74–5, *74*, *75*
Kaomise 66
Kaomise-soken 113
Karaoke bar 122
Kasa 70, *71*, *82*
Kashiwaya 12
Katayama, Haruko 99, 118
Katayama, Hiromichi 100
Katsura 40, 66, 70, 73, 77,1 24
Katsuyama 73
Kawatake III, Shinshichi 49
Kaway 83
Kazari-Dana 91
Ken 98
Ketabo 71
Kimono 17, 23, *23*, 29, *32*, 33, 38,
   38, 39, 40, 41, 43, 44, *44*, 47,
   48, *48*, 51,*51*, 52, *52*, 57, 58,
   58, 59, 62, *62*, 63, 66, *66*, 68,
   68, 69, 70, 94, 99, 100, 106,
   108, 110, 113, 116, 120, 123
Kimono, motifs 63, 66, *66*
Kimono, folding 33
Kin-byobu 38
Kin-sei era 49
Kitano 17, 89
   Odori *97*, 99, 102
   shrine 15
   Tenmangu shrine 16, 110, 113
Kiyomoto 86, 87
Kiyomoto-bushi 86
Kojiki 12
Kokyu 11
Koma 74
Komachi, Onono 111
Komon 70, 124
Komon-kimono 63, 68
Konpire-fune-fune 98
Koshoku-Ichidai-Otoko 15
Kotobuki 39
Kotobuki-kai *100*
Koto-hajime 113
Kotsuzumi 80, *83*, 84, *84*, 87, 101,
   122
Kouta 86, 87
Kurokami 44, 86
Kuro-montsuki *44*,124
Kyogen 87
Kyoho Era 86
Kyo-kotoba 34
Kyo-odori 99,102
Kyoto 6, 7, 9, 10, 12, 20, 21, 29,
   30, *30*, 32, 34, *39*, 41 44, 49,
   51, 57, 63, 70, 71, 75, 77, 81,
   83, 87, 89, 94, 95, 99, 103,

105, 106 108, 110, 113, 116, 120, 121, 122, 123
City Tourism Association 102 123
dance see Kyo Odori
Hanamachi Association 102
Prefectural Nyokoba School 81
Prefecture 13
Traditional Artistic Accomplishment Promotion Foundation 95
Kyo-Yuzen 62, 63, *63*, 124

Mae-ware wig 73
Mage 71
Make-up *37*, 40, 44, *57*, 66, 77, *77*
Mamegiku *66*
Marumage 73
Maru-obi 68
Matsuno Midori 86
Mazu 52
Meido-no-Hikyaku 49
Meiji 110
    Government 81
    Period *10*, 11, 86
    Restoration 13, 15, *15*, 44
Meoto ken 98
Mima School 81
Minamiza kabuki Theatre 16, 66, 75, 83, 113, 120
Minamoto, Shogun Yoritomo 49, 101, 111
Minamoto, Yoshinaka 111
Minamoto, Yoshitsune 49, 101, 111
Minarai 34
Minarai-jaya 23, 34, 38, 39, 41, 113
Minarai-san 18, 23, 32, 33, 124
Miokuri 40, 73
Mitarashi dango 17
Miyabi-kai 108, *108*
Miyagawa-cho 9, *9*, 102
    dance theatre 99
    hanamachi 11, 16, 17, 38, 81, 99
Miyagawa-ondo 102
Miyako dance festival 88, 89
Miyako Odori festival 73, *93*, 99, 100, 103, 108, 119, 120, 124
Miyazaki, Yuzensai 63
Mizuage 47, 124
Mizuage-danna 47
Mizu-jaya 12, 17
Mochi 75
Mochibana 75
Mokuroku *39*, 41
Monpe 119
Monten 63, *63*
Morgan, George 15
Muromachi Period 15, 91
Musical instruments 83

Naga-juban 62, 66
Nagauta 86, 87, 120, 124
Nakai 15, 23, 124
Names 34
Nara 63, 108
Nenki 47, 52,1 24
New Year Celebration 106
Ningyo-shibai 86
Ninki-Boko 81
Nishijin 16, 21, 51, 68, 102
Noh 63, 80, 84, 87, 101
Nohsatsu 70
North Field dance see Kitano Odori
Noshi-bokuro 39
Noshi-gami 40, 44, *47*
Nyokoba School 17, 106

Oamku 40
Oasobi 40
Obake 107

Obi 29, *32*, 44, 52, 62, 66, *68*, 123, 124
Obi-age 69, 125
Obi-dome 69, 125
Obi-jime 66, 68, *68, 125*
Ocha 87
Ochaya 6, 10, 13, *13*, 21, 23, *27*, *29*, 30, *32*, 33, 39, 48, 49, 51, *51*, *54*, 63, 66, 88, 92, 93, 94, 95, 96, 106, 120, 122, 125
Ochobo-guchi 77
Odori *81*, *82*, 125
Odori, Kamogawa *96*
Odori, Kitano *97*
Ofuku 73, 125
Ohana 40
Ohayashi 101
Ohikizuri 33
Oiran 49
Oiran-dochu 49
Okame 41
Okasan *18*, *20*, 21, *22*, 23, 27, 33, 38, 39, 41, 44, 47, 51, 52, 55, 92, 96, 112, 119, 120, 125
Okashi *87*
Okera flame 113
Oki 33
Okiya 11, *18*, 20, 21, 23, 30, *32*, 33, 34, 38, 39, 40, 44, 48, 51, 52, 55, 59, 63, 68, 69, 121, 125
Okobo 29, 41, 66, *69*, 70, 125
Okotousan 113
Okuni 113
Omaku 71
Omanju 99
Omatsuri 40
Omatsuri-nuke 40
Omiki see sake
Omisedashi *29*, *35*, *38*, 39, 40, 41, *41*, 44, 47, 48, 71, 125
Omote-senke 89
Onesan 20, *29*, 33, 34, 35, 38, 39, *39*, 41, 52, 77, 125
Oniisan 21, 125
Onnagata 17
Onoue school 99, 102
Onshu-kai *103*
Ooishi, Chief Retainer Kuranosuke 108
Ooishi-ki 108
Ookawa 80, 84ñ5, 87, 101, 122
Ookii-okasan 18
Ookini Foundation 102
Ookini-Zaidan 122
Ooki-onesan 38, 39
Ootsuzumi 84
Opening doors *80*, 82
Osaka 41, 86, 103
Osechi 106
Osenko 40
Otoko-geisha 49
Otokosu *18*, 23, 41, *51*, 125
Otosan 22
Otoso 106
Over-garment 68
Ozashiki 10, 122, 20, 23, 27, 73, 77, 91, 92, 93, *94*, 96, 97, 98, 108, 123, 125
Ozashiki-kago 40, 70, *70*
Ozoni 106, 113

Paulownia wood 33, 70
Pocchiri 44, 66, 69, *69*, 125
Ponto-cho 58, 101, *101*,119, 120
    dance theatre 99
    hanamachi 11, 15,*16*, 17, *18*, 38, 39, 40, 81, 89, 99, 111
    Kaburenjo *96*
    Seinen-Fujinkai 119

Rattan blinds 10, 13
Rice 55
Rice-boxes 55
Rikyu, Senno 89
Ro *59*, 62, 66, 68, 110, 125
Ryotei 93, *94*, 122–23

Sado see also Tea ceremony, 125
Sake 34, 38, 39, 96, 97, 98, 108, 120
Sakko 73, *73*, 125
Sakko hairstyle *43*, 44
Sangen 85
San-San-Kudo 34, 38, 39, 44, 55, 125
Sasage 55
Sashigami 39
Schools 79
    dance 99
    Fujima 99, 102
    Hanayagi 99, 102
    Inoue 99, 100, 101, 106, 113, 118
    Nyokoba 106
    Onoue 99, 102
    Wakayagi 99,102
Senja-fuda 70
Senju-iwai 40
Senninbari 120
Setsubun 73, 107
Sha 62, 68, 125
Shacho-san 22
Shado 87, 88
Shamisen 6, 48, 80, *83*, 85, *85*, 86, 87, *87*, 92, 97, 101, 122, 123, 125
Shassan 22
Shemidaiko 84
Shibori 62
Shidashi 23
Shijo bridge 63
Shijo Street 13
Shikomi 32
Shikomi-san 32, 33, 33, 34, 47, 125
Shimabara 49
    haidan 120
    hanamachi *10*, *11*, 12, *12*, 80, *80*, 81
Shimada wig 73
Shimai 87
Shinbashi Enbujo Theatre 100
Shinbashi-dori 9
Shintoism 105, 120
Shiraba 83
Shirabyoshi 49, 87, 111
Shironuri 33, 125
Shochu 97
Shodo 125
Shoin-zukuri 91
Shoji 91
Shomyo 87
Shosoin 113
Showa Period 55, 70, 73
Shrine maiden 16
Sinobu Koi 86
Sisters 34, 35, 38, 39, 41, 48
Soba 108, *112*, 113
Soji day 40
Soji-nuke 40
Soken 113
Sugatari 86
Sugawara, Minister Michazane 16
Sugoroku 12
Sumiya 11

Tabi 40, 69, *70*, 125
Tachikata 83, 125
Taiko *79*, 83-4, 101
Taiko-joro 49

Taiko-mochi 49
Taira, Premier Kiyomori 49
Taisho period *30*, 44, 70
Takarabune 41
Takizawa, Bakin 12
Tama-kan 73
Tamaryo 123
Tan 58, 125
Tang Dynasty 63
Tanizaki, Jun-ichiro 120
Tansu 33
Tatami 6, 10, 125
    mats *32*, 82
    room 33
Tayu *10*, 11, 12, *12*, 49, 86, 125
Tea ceremony 33, *87*, 88–9, *88*, *89*, 99, 106, 108, 113
Teachers 83
Teahouse 18, *21*, *22*, 23, 93, 94, 95, 99, 108, 110, *110*, 112, 113, 115, 120
Tenpyo Era 63
Tenugui *39*
Tokaidochu *Hizakurige*34
Tokiwazu 86, 87, 120
Tokiwazu-bushi 86
Tokonoma 6, 10, 38, 88, 96, 125
Tokugawa, Shogun Ieyasu 110
Tokyo 40, 49, 52, 86, 100, 103
    1923 earthquake 118
Tomimoto II, Itsukidayu 86
Tosenkyo 12
Toyotomi, Shogun Hideyoshi 15, 17, 89
Training 32–3
Tsubushi-shimada wig 73
Tsuzumi 83

Uchiwa 75
Umekawa 49
Umenimo Haru 86
Ura-senke 89
Utai 87
Utaimono 87

Wachigai ya 11
Waka 111, *111*
Wakashu kabuki 16
Wakayagi school 99, 102
Ware-shinobu 39, 71, 73, *73*, 125
Wars
    China 13
    Russia 13
    World War One 13, 116
    World War Two 116, 118, 120
Washi 91
Wataboshi 15

Yado-no-sakae 108
Yago 17
Yakata 21
Yakko-shimada 73
Yakyu ken 98
Yamashina 108
Yasaka Nyokoba Gakuen 18
Yasaka Nyokoba School *80*, 81
Yasaka shrine 12, 15, *15*, 16, 108, *108*, 113
Yatushashi 49
Yogaku 6
Yoshii, Isamu 111, 112, 113, 120
Yoshiwara 49
Yukata 58, *58*, 62, 70, 108, 125
Yukata-kai 102
Yuzen-Nagashi 63

Zori 62, 66, 70
Zuiki festival 110, *110*

Acknowledgements

The author would like to thank the following individuals and organizations
for their help in the production of this book:

Ochaya (Tea houses)

Ishihatsu (Miyagawa-cho)

Iyuki (Ponto-cho)

Kaden (Miyagawa-cho)

Nakazato (Kamishichiken)

Tomio (Gion-Kobu)

Okiya (Lodging house)

Sawada (Ponto-cho)

Geiko

Koito (Miyagawa-cho)

Mai (Gion-Kobu)

Mameyoshi (Ponto-cho)

Miyoji (Ponto-cho)

Momoko (Former Geiko/Gion-Kobu)

Shinatoshi (Ponto-cho)

Umeharu (Kamishichiken)

Maiko

Fukuaya (Miyagawa-cho)

Naohiro (Kamishichiken)

Naoyuki (Kamishichiken)

Rinya (Ponto-cho)

Individuals:

Fumika Tamura

Kanako Sakai

Kinu Shigeyama

Kojiro Sakai

The author also wishes to thank Michiko Kurita for kindly
introducing her to Carlton Books through the Frances Kelly agency.

Shops & Studios

Ikuoka-ya (Hair accessories & Kyoto-Souvenirs)

Kanazen (Japanese musical instruments)

Kintake-do (Hair accessories)

Kyo-Katsura Imanishi (Wigs)

Minochu (Foot wear)

Okazen (Kimono)

Tsujikura-Shoten (Umbrellas and lanterns)

Yamato-Biyoshitsu (Hair-maker)

Schools, Organizations and Newspapers

Foundation for the Promotion of Traditional Artistic
Accomplishments (Ookini Zaidan)

Gion Kobu Association

Kamishichiken Kenban

Kyoto Shimbun Newspaper Co.,Ltd.

Yasaka Nyokoba Gakuen

Assistance in translation:

Janet Counsell

Additional references:

Gion – Tanko-sha 1995

Gion Mai Goyomi – Kyoto Shoin 1992

Gion Maiko Saijiki – Toho Shuppan 1995

Gion Maiko Sho – Yoshimura Shobo 1978

Japonica (Encyclopedia) – Shogakukan 1969

Kyo Mai – Kyoto Shimbun Newspaper/Tanko Shinsya 1960

Kyo Maiko – Kyoto Shoin 1987

Kyoto Jiten – Kyodo Shuppan 1979

Kyoto-no-Nenju-Gyoji – by Kinosuke Usui,
Hoikusha 1968

Kyoto-no-Rekishi – Gakugei Shorin 1968

Kyoto-no-Wana – by Akira Shigeyama and Haruki Kamata, *KK Best
Sellers* 1997

Kyoto Yukaku Kenbunroku – by Yasuhiko Tanaka /
Kyo-wo-Kataru-kai 1993

Sakariba-no-Girei-kenkyu – by Kayo Ohgaki

Photographs:

The publishers would like to thank the following sources for their
kind permission to reproduce the pictures in this book:

All photography courtesy of Kyoko Aihara apart from:-
Kyo-wo-Kataru-Kai 10, 14; Kyoto Prefectural Sohgoh Siryokan
Collection, photo: Suizan Kurokawa 31; Fujika 42, 44, 45, 50, 51r;
Kyoto Shimbun 86, 92–93, 96, 97, 109; Tony Stone/Paul Chesley
118l, 121, 122; Koito 118r

Every effort has been made to acknowledge correctly and contact
the source and/copyright holder of each picture, and Carlton Books
Limited apologises for any unintentional errors or omissions which
will be corrected in future editions of this book.